Iran: Progenitor of the New Cold War

By

Michael W. Schnorr PhD

authorHOUSE™

1663 LIBERTY DRIVE, SUITE 200
BLOOMINGTON, INDIANA 47403
(800) 839-8640
WWW.AUTHORHOUSE.COM

First published by AuthorHouse 02/04/05

ISBN: 1-4208-1573-3 (sc)
ISBN: 1-4208-1574-1 (dj)

Printed in the United States of America
Bloomington, Indiana

This book is printed on acid-free paper.

Introduction

In the days immediately following the heinous and unprovoked attacks on American citizens, the western media scrambled for so-called experts in terrorism, middle-eastern studies, and Islam. Many of us were glued to our televisions, mesmerized by the continuous re-play of horrible scenes of September 11, 2001 – scenes that to this day cultivate a sense of hatred and misunderstanding of the middle-eastern culture. Further more, 9/11 invoked a renewed sense of urgency with regard to Iran and their often radicalized Muslim views. In *Iran: Progenitor of the New Cold War,* Dr. Michael Schnorr details a remarkably insightful study focused on the Iranian threat not merely with regard to Israel, but to Western society at large.

At the time of this writing, the radical Shiite Cleric Moqtada al Sadr is hole up in the Imam Ali Shrine in Najaf, Iraq. This shrine represents the third holiest city on the planet, behind Mecca and Medina in Saudi Arabia. Al Sadr's militia supported by Iranian interests has approximately 1,000 insurgents inside the cemetery and mosque and have refused to surrender. Thus, multi-national forces and the Iraqi National Guard are reluctantly forced to engage their enemy in a volatile and potentially world-opinion shaping battle. If one studies the history of this unpredictable region, it is transparent to those well-informed that "world opinion," directly impacts our global inter-play, politics, and diplomacy – as Dr. Schnorr so eloquently highlights, this is ever so true with regard to Iran. As we send young men and women into battle, perhaps we shouldn't forget the real fight may be due east.

During a recent visit to Israel, I had a lengthy dinner discussion with Dr. Martin Kramer, a Washington Institute Ira Weiner Fellow, regarding Iran's nuclear weapons proliferation and the growing threat to Israel. Dr. Kramer, a former Professor of Middle Eastern Studies at Tel Aviv University, left an indelible mark on my view of Islam and the greater Muslim community as a whole. Scholars and diplomats the world over have written volumes on the threat to world order that Iran represents. As Dr. Schnorr outlines in his seminal work, the threat is REAL! The case of Iran is much more dangerous and deleterious than Iraq. With the benefit of hind-site, there is little doubt that Iraq's intentions in invading Kuwait in 1990 were mainly economic and political. Iraq had been until April 2003, a dictatorial regime with secular orientation and aims. Conversely, Iran is a fundamentalist Muslim State with outspoken hostile intentions towards the West. Perhaps more unsettling is Iran is a known supporter of international terrorism.

Iran has long been considered the pioneer of the Islamic fundamentalism phenomenon in the 20th century. Shortly after 9/11, a time when our attention was rightly diverted, intelligence reports and satellite pictures appeared in the Islamic newspaper, Yediot Aharonot, (September 26, 2001). Multiple intelligence sources had confirmed a marked increase in Iranian efforts to develop a nuclear plant for military purposes. As events unfolded and weeks turned into months, months into years, we knew Iran was encroaching on the ability to develop nuclear technologies. Their success largely depends on support from sympathetic neighboring nation-states, corrupt oil-rich companies, foreign aid and scientific expertise.

When asked "how long do you think it will take Iran to develop a nuclear weapon?" Dr. Kramer indicated "less than 2 years." My God, less than two years? How can that be? Simply stated, Iran maintained contacts and friendly clandestine relationships. They sought critical information from various European countries and the Chinese government for many years before the United States applied overwhelming diplomatic pressures forcing the Iranian's to cease and desist. However, Iran wasn't about to merely acquiesce and quickly turned their attention toward Russia and their experienced nuclear scientist pool.

Current intelligence reports place Iran's nuclear warhead completion at 2-3 years. Yet, this timeline potentially might be shortened if Iran is successful in obtaining atomic components, equipment, and production protocols from myriad black markets and rogue scientists. Many analysts also suggest that Iran is developing surface-to-surface missiles capable of carrying nuclear, biological, and chemical warheads which easily range much of Europe and the Middle East.

As I listened to Dr. Kramer's poignant analysis, attempting to digest his theories, I was perplexed as to why the free world chooses to exercise naiveté regarding the true Iranian threat to world-order. In light of the terror attack on the pentagon and twin towers, western countries would be wise to treat any Muslim fundamentalist country as a direct threat to its national security. When nations act to protect their citizens and sovereignty from nuclear threats, many are quick to condemn the action as illegal or immoral. As was the case when Israel attacked and destroyed a nuclear weapons plant in Iraq, many voices, American and Western European, openly condemned Israel for conducting the attack. Had Israel failed to act, the United States' led coalition in the first Gulf War may have experienced a completely different military and diplomatic scenario in August 1990, the month that Saddam Hussein's forces invaded their neighbor Kuwait.

Unquestionably, Iran is a member of the web of terror and their insistence on building a nuclear weapon is alarming. The moment President Jimmy Carter allowed the overthrow of the Shah of Iran, radicalism spawned by Ayatollah Khomeini flourished. Iran was no longer considered an ally of America. The 1978-1979 Iranian revolution set in motion the creation of the first Islamic fundamentalist state. Almost 25 years later, we still struggle with developing the best course of action for containing Iran. While our diplomats weigh options and our military strategists develop operation plans, Iran is anything but quiescent. Led by those who toppled the Shah, Iran has become a leading exporter of radical Islam and a leading supporter of Islamist terrorism.

Dr. Schnorr's compelling research has produced not simply a remarkable work but an awakening of our collective conscience. He leads us down a shadowy path of deception, terrorism, and proliferation that shows Iran continues to spawn a crafty web of ill-intentions toward the West. Defeating this increasingly dangerous threat may mean overthrowing the regime. The modern free world must act quickly to denounce Iran's weapons of mass destruction production. In addition, even if Iran officially ends its nuclear weapons development program, it is unlikely that the mullahs will cease fighting, training, and funding terror groups around the world. Now that Dr. Schnorr has brilliantly recounted the seriousness of the Iranian threat, the remaining question, therefore, is how to deal with Iran and effect regime change. Change, we know, is fundamentally never easy. It may require cultivating the growing support of domestic resistance to the mullahs, diplomatic pressures, and military force. Before our administration takes one more step with regard to Iran, they would be wise to read *Iran: Progenitor of the New Cold War*.

Professor Steven J. Greer
American Military University
August 2004

"In a nuclear duel in the region, Israel may kill 100 million Muslims. Muslims can sustain such casualties knowing that in exchange, there would be no Israel on the map".

Hashemi Rafsanjani

Former Iranian President[1]

"Iran has been a supporter of al Qaeda from 1993 to 1996, during which time al Qaeda was based in Sudan. The Iranian security services [IRGC] and the MOIS [Ministry of Information and Security] supported a number of terrorist camps during the period al Qaeda was in Khartoum."

Rohan Gunaratna

Noted Expert on al Qaeda[2]

" Can we withstand America's threats and domineering attitude with a policy of Détente? Can we foil dangers coming from America through dialogue of civilizations? Will we be able to protect the Islamic Republic from international Zionism by signing conventions banning the proliferation of chemical and nuclear weapons".

Yahya Rahim Safavi

Commanding Officer

Iranian IRGC[3]

"Possessing technology for the nuclear fuel cycle is our right and nobody can deny us of this right under international regulations. We will continue cooperation with the IAEA as long as our interests require and as long as we know various plots led by the US are ineffective"

Ardakani (Ali) Khatami

President of the Islamic Republic[4]

"No comparable oil-rich nation has ever engaged, or would be engaged, in this set of activities -- or would pursue them for nearly two decades behind a continuing cloud of secrecy and lies to the IAEA inspectors and the international community -- unless it was dead set on building nuclear weapons".

> John R. Bolton,
> US Under Secretary for Arms Control and International Security
> June 24, 2004
> Testifying before the House International Relations Committee[5]

"...Iran, for decades, not months or a few years, but for decades has been designated by our government as a principal sponsor of state terrorism...I want to add it is *the* principal...if there is one country, above all, that has taken a primary role in sponsoring the terrorist organizations around the world, it is Iran. If we are going to defeat worldwide Islamic Fundamentalist terrorism we must make the government of Iran change its policy..."

> Steve Pomerantz,
> Former Head of FBI CT
> Fox News June 22, 2004[6]

If Iran goes nuclear, you worry that Hezbollah goes nuclear." When you have a nation that actively supports terrorism and seeks nuclear weapons, "you cannot rule out the possibility" that it could collaborate with terrorists "to carry out nuclear violence."

> Paul Leventhal,
> President of the Nuclear Control Institute[7]

Table of Contents

Chapter One
The Threat of Terrorism and Nuclear Proliferation in the Persian Gulf

The threat and danger of nuclear war is more apparent now than at any other time in history. The proliferation of nuclear technology by rogue states that have the intent of using the knowledge to develop a nuclear weapon is at an all time high. Nowhere in the world is this more prominent than in Iran.

Iran is actively seeking and receiving support, technology, hardware and training to establish its own nuclear facilities. The dual use technology, the technology that can be used for peaceful nuclear power and the development of a nuclear weapon that is so common on the international market today, is being used by Iran and perhaps by Syria to develop its nuclear weapons. North Korea has followed this path and has developed nuclear weapons with the intent on using them to blackmail and or attack the US and its interests. Or perhaps use them to fuel other rogue states and their nuclear projects. Despite ongoing talks, the North Koreans intent concerning nuclear weapons is unclear.

The proliferation of nuclear weapons has been an international relations issue for more than fifty years. United States, Russia, China, France, Israel,

India and Pakistan all possess and are ready to use nuclear weapons if threatened. Other countries such as Iran, Syria, Uzbekistan, Turkey and up until recently, Iraq have all been attempting to acquire nuclear weapons or the means to produce the weapons themselves. Iran appears to be the closest to attaining nuclear power and possibly a military application of the technology.

The acquisition of nuclear weapons by Iran in the near future will push the global community into a New Cold War. The elements that were so common during the First Cold War are present and escalating to the point that Cold War II is a reality right now. Iran is pressing forward in its desire to acquire first nuclear power, and then by using dual purpose technology will be able to develop nuclear weapons.

With approximately 10% of the explored oil reserves, Iran sits in a strategic location that will be a point of contention in the coming years. Pursing its agenda to acquire nuclear weapons, Iran could easily dominate the Persian Gulf and plunge the world into an economic cataclysm that could split alliances and drive countries to war.

The continuing policies of the Islamic Revolutionary government in Iran have changed the face of the Middle East since its inception in 1979. With the deposing of the Shah, Iranian Militants were able to seize control and change the course of the Middle East.

Relations with the US have been cut off since 1979 and Iran has publicly stated it is inevitable that the two countries will engage in armed confrontation. While most feel this will be through the military, there are several indications that Cold War II has already begun with the nuclear proliferation states such as Iran and Libya in one corner and the Nuclear Containment states such as the US and the UK in another corner. The undecided countries such as France, Germany, Russia and Canada find themselves placed in a category of appeasers.

With the stage set for a political/cultural/military confrontation, it is only a matter of time before the people of the world realize that we are involved in the Second Cold War. The significance of which is tremendous – in money, manpower and possibly serious casualties.

The Iranian government has a nuclear program that is very well developed and it is speculated that it will be able develop a nuclear weapon within the next 6-18 months. Once that happens, the Persian Gulf will be controlled by the Islamic militant government of Iran and will control a majority of the explored oil reserves in the world. Headlines such as "Oil Prices rise 500%", "Shi'a Mullahs claim Persian Gulf as Iranian Territory", "US economy plunged into depression" will dominate the media.

A nuclear weapon in the hands of individuals who are willing to use it for mass destruction and terror is a danger to the world. Terror organizations supported by Iran include al Qaeda, Hamas, Hezbollah and Islamic Jihad. A detonation of a weapon in Tel Aviv, London, New York, Los Angeles, or Paris would kill millions and severely cripple the international economy. It would take decades to recover economically from just one detonation. The estimated loss directly related to the September 11, 2001 attacks was $680 billion.[8] Should the Islamic Militants detonate a second weapon, the modern society we know would be drastically changed for the worst.

"Atomic weapon development assures mutual destruction", "Russians are uncooperative at bargaining table" "Soviets develop missile capable of Striking Europe and Middle East". These type of headlines haunted the US and Western Europe through the Cold War and struck fear into every peace loving government in the world. However, these headlines with slight alterations could be the news of tomorrow. Replace "Russians" with "Islamic Militants" and "Soviets" with "Iranian Islamic fundamentalists" and it becomes clear that the Persian Gulf is the setting for the next cold war.

Most Americans view the Global War on Terror (GWOT) as a distant war fought in Afghanistan and Iraq, but the effects of the war are being felt at home. Not by just the casualties of war, but by the international politics and relations with Europe, Central Asia, Russia, China, Indonesia, and other countries that are involved. As the US economy continues to improve, the delicate balance of international trade, exports, economic power of the dollar, interest rates and international events all come into play. If the balance of power in the Persian Gulf is disrupted, the Western powers will feel the economic stranglehold Iran will have on the world due to the West's dependence on oil and the volatile nature of the Middle East.

Cold War II has already begun and the world is heading for a show down in Iran – very soon. The Iranians have already stated that they feel war with the US is inevitable and have developed war plans and defenses based on the use of nuclear weapons. To counter this growing atomic force in the Persian Gulf; American projection of power, prevention, preemption and intervention are necessary.

The acquisition of nuclear weapons by Iran in the near future will push the global community into a new level in the GWOT. Cold War II and the GWOT are directly linked through the actions of the Islamic Revolutionary Government of Iran. Iran's desire for nuclear weapons and its desire to sponsor and fund terrorists that attack the US are two major elements that prove Iran is the enemy.

In the past, during the first Cold War, the US and USSR were the primary powers that had obtained nuclear weapons. With ideologies so far apart that nuclear war seemed inevitable, the Cold War was won without nuclear disaster. China was able to obtain the nuclear technology in the 1950's and develop its own nuclear arsenal. But with China's fundamental political break from the USSR over its interpretation of communism, the Cold War became a world event in a three-sided arena. For almost 50 years, the world was at the brink of nuclear war and the economies and political boundaries of the countries under the influence of the nuclear spheres were directly affected. In the 1950s, individual citizens actually built fallout shelters on their own property due to the fear of nuclear war. Many buildings in the US were designated as fallout shelters. Evacuation plans were drawn up and civil defense was the order of the day.

The economy of the world was affected directly by the Cold War and it has been estimated that the US alone spent over $8 Trillion from 1946 to 1996 on nuclear weapons for the Cold War.[9] The economy was stable and continued to grow in the West, but behind the Iron Curtain it was dismal. It is estimated that the USSR spent approximately 50% of the total national product on defense. The USSR had a closed money system and was dependent on the influx of foreign currency. With little to export besides caviar and vodka, the Soviets and then the Chinese found a lucrative business in the arms trade. Simple small arms and complex weapons systems were offered on the international market with the AK47 rifle being the most exported weapon in the history of the world- over 30 million sold. Rebellions, revolutions, insurrections and wars were funded and supported by all sides during the Cold War. The Soviets in their race to strengthen and expand their borders devoted most of their GNP to funding and developing the military and the political base in the Soviet Union and its satellite communist countries such as Poland, Czechoslovakia, Hungary, Romania, Albania and Yugoslavia, not to forget East Germany.

The US won the Cold War with the fall of the Soviet Union, not because of military might, but because to the brilliance and fortitude of Ronald Reagan. His vision of the USSR as an evil empire and confronting it with the strongest weapon the US has: its capitalist-based economy was the most effective indirect method of toppling the USSR. Once the US- sponsored space-borne anti-missile system designated the Strategic Defense Initiative (SDI) was introduced and then deemed feasible, the leaders of the USSR realized that the immense sums of money, technology and manpower that had been invested in their nuclear weapons program was for naught. Their nuclear missile systems were obsolete. The well-known nuclear paradigm – the threat of mutual destruction- was broken. If it were to come to war, the US had the capability of launching nuclear weapons and in turn would be able to shoot down or destroy the Soviet nuclear response. The Soviets had no choice but to negotiate with the West and try to regain the initiative. In the Soviets eyes, a solution had to be found to counter SDI. But research and development requires money- a large amount of money that the USSR did not have. One of the ways to obtain money in the past had been to divert money from the economy -- money that wasn't there. The Soviet economy had been suppressed for so long, there was nothing more to take. The Soviet leadership realized this too late and the Soviet Union as an ideology failed.

The Soviet Union no longer exists, though many of the nuclear weapons and weapon systems still do. Several countries that had traded with the USSR in the 70s and 80s are still ready to use the anti-aircraft missiles, the AK-47s and Rocket Propelled Grenades (RPG). In this respect, though controversial, in the right hands, the weapons themselves are not dangerous but in the wrong hands, they are deadly. The weapons are not the cause of the problem of violence in the world. The people ready to use them are. The ideology behind mass destruction via the nuclear detonation is a danger. The USSR and the US both had used this ideology during the first Cold War. Today there are others that wish to destroy the US with this ideology. Who is behind this ideology? Although some would disagree, Islamic Militants possess an ideology that seeks weapons of mass destruction, ideally, nuclear weapons to inflict as many casualties as possible in the United States.

Nuclear technology exists in many parts of the world today. Most countries that seek nuclear capability for energy use also have developed the weapons as well. South Africa has been the only country to dismantle its nuclear program, including its weapons program. Dismantling a nuclear program of a rogue nation into today's volatile international scene is possible, but complicated. While nuclear energy has a benefit to the civilian energy production sector of the economy, the capability of wielding a nuclear weapon in the face of an enemy to show strength has been the goal of several nations including the USSR, China, India, Pakistan, presumably Israel, North Korea and the United States. Iran wants to wield nuclear weapons to destroy its enemy – the US and Israel

Iran and the Islamic Revolution are a danger to the US and the world. The ideology of the government is the danger as it seeks to acquire nuclear weapons. The government has an active nuclear program that has been disclosed to the IAEA, but there have been major discrepancies found in their program that would suggest a covert parallel program is ongoing with the goal of building nuclear weapons. The Islamic Revolutionary government in Iran is not only a danger to the international community, but also a direct threat to its own citizens. Millions in Iran are oppressed and thousands killed and tortured each year.

The Iranian dilemma is complicated, but it is clear that the path that Supreme Leader Ayatollah Ali Hoseini Khameini and the Mullahs of the Guardian Counsel (the leaders of the Iranian government) have chosen is a danger to the world in several ways.

The number one danger is nuclear proliferation. The creation a nuclear state that would dominate the Persian Gulf and the oil exporters of the area is a danger. Another international concern and direct threat to the citizens of the world is Iran's blatant sponsorship of Mid East terrorism.

Iran is also dangerous because of its ties to international terrorism that is being proliferated throughout the world through the efforts of the IRGC and their attempts to export the Islamic Revolution. Iran is a danger to the world due to its alliance with North Korea and the free trade of weapons, technology and training of personnel.

In regards to these two aspects of Iranian foreign policy, the notion that Iran is not a danger to the US and rest of the world is unfounded. News was released on June 25, 2004 on the Fox news channel that the Iranians have resumed their uranium enrichment process. This action is in protest by the western powers, the UN and IAEA, however, Iran continues to pursue its goal of nuclear power. The enriched uranium can be used in dual use technology that can be used in both power plants and nuclear weapons.

The power of the Iranian government is based on the Sharia Islamic Law, which is the strict application of Islam law into daily life. The mullahs maintain control over the people and do not share their power with others including the Iranian President. President Khatami heads the so-called government and was popularly elected. The Guardian Counsel was appointed by Ayatollah Khomeini and when a replacement is needed, its members are appointed to the counsel rather than elected. The Guardian Counsel holds the power in Iran. Khatami is merely a figure-head. President Khatami wants to decentralize the political power of the government so the mullahs do not have such overwhelming power. This has been met with great support from the population, but also strong condemnation by the Mullahs. So the question of nuclear power and the Iranian government come down to: what are the nuclear weapons going to be used for? And if the government does control these weapons, how will this benefit them?

The Iranian government has several options to pursue with nuclear weapons; the Iranians can blackmail the west by threatening to use the weapon, they can also export the weapon or several smaller weapons to its allies Hezbollah and Hamas. But a more dangerous situation is exporting the nuclear weapons for training or development in the Sudan terrorist camps where a dirty bomb or a nuclear device can be assembled. The technology is present, the training would be adequate, and the willingness is overwhelming. Once the methods and materials are available, it is only a matter of time before the terrorists use a weapon. Because al Qaeda and the other terrorist organizations that are supported by Iran share the camps and have contact with each other, it is only a matter of time before al Qaeda obtains the methods and technology. If this occurs, they have already stated they intend to use a weapon of mass destruction - a nuclear device will be detonated in the West.

What are the motivations of the Iranians in seeking nuclear weapons? Do the Mullahs want to export this technology or do they want in their possession a nuclear weapon? The angle that they are attempting to pursue is one of power. They wish to maintain power and export the Islamic revolution ideology to unite Shi'a Muslims worldwide.

The Persian Gulf region is important not only for the oil production and export, but also it is a strategic location. It is politically, economically and strategically important. Other oil exporters include Russia, Venezuela, Mexico, Brazil and Central Asia as well as others. As the largest nation in the Gulf area, major developments on the international level will have wide repercussions throughout the area and beyond. Iran has a direct supply of fuel and is a major player in the regional socio-political scene.

Some of the roots of the first Cold War include distrust and confrontation. The real motivator for the Cold War was fear. The USSR was intensely fearful of another war. In WWII and several years preceding it, over 40 million Soviet citizens were killed. The purges by Stalin's CHEKA secret police and the Nazi invasion of the Soviet Union in WWII are still remembered with tearful accounts today. Fear of another cataclysmic war on their soil motivated the Soviets to dominate Eastern Europe and any other area they could influence.

Iran had been involved in the devastating war of the 1980s with Iraq and lost over 1 million people. It was the most costly and damaging war in the region. The people have an intense fear of another devastating war and the Iranian government feels that it would be justified in using nuclear weapons to avoid the long drawn out destruction that it experienced in the Iran-Iraq war.

But Iran is only a part of the problem. The terrorist organizations that it supports and promulgates are a danger as well. Hamas, Hezbollah and Islamic Jihad will, without a doubt, use the nuclear devices provided by Iran on Israel and the US. al Qaeda has also declared that it will use nuclear weapons on the "infidels" in its quest for a Pan-Islamic World. The ruthlessness of the Islamic militants and terrorists is well known and remembered with the grisly decapitations of Daniel Pearl, Nicholas Berg and others. Equally horrendous is the random killing of civilians and school children in homicide bombings and shootings.

The next major attack in the US will be greater than that of 9/11 and may involve several nuclear weapons. On at least one occasion, al Qaeda has boasted that it has in its possession suitcase nukes and will use them against the US.[10] The US government also considers this a distinct possibility and Homeland Security is taking precautions to monitor the areas of large cities with nuclear detection devices.

So why does the government of Iran want to pursue a nuclear program and presumably develop nuclear weapons? In one word – power. Political and economic power in the Persian Gulf. They want to be taken seriously in the international community and they feel that nuclear power will give them that prestige. The underlying reason to have a nuclear power program is to covertly build the infrastructure for a nuclear weapon production facility. There are many facets to the Islamic Republic's motivations for obtaining nuclear power. The Shi'a Islamic beliefs tied to Iran's government and its vehement hatred of the US and Israel along with the quest for international power are two facets that will be discussed later.

Chapter Two
Islam – Sunni, Shia, Wahabi,

Islam is a major influence in the culture of Iran and surrounding countries. There are two major divisions of Islam in Iran which are Shi'a and Sunni. A third type of Islam that is practiced in Saudi Arabia is called Wahabism. Shi'a Islam is the dominant religion in Iran with the government officials all being Shi'a. Approximately 8% of the population in Iran follows Sunni Islam. [11]

The Sunnis believe in five pillars of faith and they do not accept the doctrine of the Imamate or successor to Muhammed to be more than just a political leader. The Shi'a Muslims believe in seven pillars of faith, which include the five that the Sunnis believe plus *the Jihad* and *the requirement to do good works and avoid all evil thoughts, words and deeds*. They also believe that the Imam is more than just a political leader. The Imam must be a spiritual leader as well, and be able to interpret the inner mysteries of the Qur'an and the Sharia. Shi'a Muslims revere Ali Ibn Abi Talib [cousin of the Prophet] as the first Imam and his descendents, including his sons. The Mosque of Ali is located in Najaf, Iraq and is a flashpoint for the Shi'as. The line continues to the Twelfth Imam who is believed to have ascended and will return to earth on judgement day. [12]The Sunnis believe that the Imam is a political leader only.

Understanding Islam

There are several sects in Islam which include Sunni, Shi'a, Wahabis, Sufis and Salafis and each claims to be following the authentic tradition of the Prophet Mohammed. The Prophet Mohammed and the Quran are very explicit in explaining that only one Islamic Sect is the correct one. However, he did not just come out and state that Sunni or Wahabi or Shi'a Islam is the correct version. Mohammed explained that Judaism and Christianity up to that point had split into numerous sects. He further explained that if Islam followed the same path, the only group that would go to paradise would be the one to which the Prophet Mohammed and his followers belonged. The major players of Islam, mentioned above, all feel that theirs is the correct group and differ on several items of interest.

Defining Islam in the context of today's society requires an understanding of the religion and the ideology behind it. Islam is one of three major religions that have spread from the Middle East to the West. Christianity and Judaism are the other two major religions. The Islamic faith has spread to all corners of the Globe including a large population in the United States. Major Islamic population centers include the Middle East and Malaysia.

Christianity and Islam

The Muslim religion has a long and rich history starting with its founder Mohammed in the 7th Century of the Common Era (CE). It has, unfortunately at times, been at odds with the West resulting in several long and bloody wars that have been fought between Christianity and Islam. To some, this history of differing opinions, has become a basis for the modern turmoil in the Middle East.

Over 1.3 billion people in the world right now are Muslim and share a history of the religion over the past 14 centuries. Indeed, it had been the dominant religion in the world from the 7th to 18th Century CE. Through military conquest and expansion, Muhammad and his followers dominated

Arabia and then the area from Morocco to India. Through the centuries, Islam has spread from Spain to Indonesia; Kazakhstan to Senegal. The religion has been marked by great kingdoms with a diverse industry and commerce as well as its original and creative sciences.[13]

However, in October 732 CE, French foot soldiers on the Loire River defeated the Muslim army that had crossed the Pyrenees Mountains from Spain. The Muslims had enjoyed great conquest up to this point under the leadership of Abderrahman. Against all odds, Charles Martel and his men battled the Muslim army and defeated it in what has become known as the Battle of Tours. This battle stopped the northern advance of Islam into Europe. [14]In the following centuries, battles over the Middle East and especially in Constantinople occurred resulting in the Crusades. In the 14th Century the Ottoman Empire resumed their attack on Europe in the name of Islam. Most of the borders remained essentially the same until the beginning of WWI and the 20th Century.

Christianity and Islam Clash

There has been no other event in history that has demonstrated the areas of difference between Islam and Christianity than the Crusades. In 1095, the Pope, fearing that the Muslims were interfering with the Christian pilgrims in Jerusalem, asked the kings of Europe to save Jerusalem by capturing it from the Muslims. He promised to forgive their sins for their trouble. The kings of France, Germany England and Hungary responded with a military force that crushed the unprepared Muslims and the Europeans captured Jerusalem.

The Crusaders killed the all inhabitants of the city whether they were Muslim or Christian. The Crusaders then physically occupied the city and plundered its riches. They continued their campaign and captured other Muslim cities and the killing continued. The Europeans had captured the Holy City for the Pope and established effective rule over the territory stretching from southern Turkey to the border of Egypt.

13

However, the combined armies of the Crusader Kings did not always get along. During the rule of the disunited Crusaders, a Muslim sultan named Saladin rose to power in Syria. He was able to unite several Muslim regions under his banner and fought a vicious campaign to liberate the conquered territories. After the decisive battle at Hattin in Syria in 1187, he was able to finally force the surrender of Jerusalem in 1192.

The Crusaders attempted seven more times to recapture the Holy Land, but by 1270 the Christians had decided to resume their pilgrimage to the city rather than continue the fight. The centuries of fighting in and around Jerusalem have left a lasting impression of the Christian Crusaders on the Islamic and Arabic culture. Presumably because the Islamic militants of today identify with the military establishment of Saladin , the goal of expelling the foreigners from Islamic lands has its roots in the horribly bloody Crusader campaigns. [15]

Wahabis

Wahabism is based on the controversial teachings of Abd al-Wahab, a 'rebel' against the traditional Islamic teachings. In the mid 18th century, Wahab, who was known for his brief writings and teachings on his version of Islam, made an alliance with Muhammad b. Sa'ud who pledged to aid Abd al-Wahab in waging jihad against all those who deviated from his understanding of the *tauhid*. The Tauhid of Allah means "both the oneness and uniqueness of Allah Most High". Tauhid means attributing/ ascribing/dedicating all attributes, beliefs and forms of worship to Allah and allowing none of these to be toward other than Allah Most High. The Tauhid is divided into three areas. These areas are common to the Sunni, the Shia and the Wahabi, but the interpretation of the last one is the area of contention.

Tauhid Ar-Ruboobiya. The exclusiveness of Allah as omnipotent lord.

Tauhid Ar-Uloohiya. The exclusive uniqueness of Allah as deity.

Tauhid Ar-Asmaa' wa As-Sifaat. The exclusive uniqueness of Allah with regard to His names and attributes as He told (the Umma – the Muslim community) in the Qur'an or commanded the Prophet to tell (the Umma) in the hadith. [16]

It is the third tauhid that the Wahabis say should only be between the worshiper and Allah. Such a violation of the third tauhid takes place in any act involving any entity other than the worshipper and God. No clerics, no Mullahs, no mention of the Prophet Mohammed, no assistance from anyone in spiritual matters pertaining to Islam are permitted per the third tauhid. [17]This belief has caused a major problem in the interpretation of the word of Allah in Islam. In 1922 the House of Saud took control of Arabia and made Wahabi Islam the national religion because it was deemed the purest form of the religion. This idea and practice of Islam has alienated the Saudi Kingdom from the Sunni and Shi'a Islam. The Saudi government today exports fossil fuels to the West and employs foreigners in their country which is key to their existence. The Saudis believe this is necessary and are at odds with other Muslim countries. However, they believe that this conduct does not violate their religion - as the individual Muslim and Allah have a religious relationship despite the foreign presence. The actions of the Saudi government in reference to its close relationship with its Western allies and the fact that they allow the Western 'Crusading' armies into the land of Mecca and Medina has been seen as being almost traitorous in the Islamic world. This has divided the Persian Gulf socially and theologically. Because the religion of Islam is a major institution within the government, and in some countries, is the government, the interpretation of the religion has divided the Gulf politically as well.

The idea that the foreigners have returned to the Arab lands to invade, destroy, reshape the governments and colonize the Holy Land is a current belief that has its roots in the Medieval Crusades. The Crusades marked the beginning of a centuries old conflict between Christianity and Islam. While the Sunnis, Shias and Wahabis are at odds theocratically, they will not hesitate to work together against a common enemy. This is being discovered in the Global War on Terror. However, the Sunnis and Shias have more in common than their Wahabi counterparts and there have been several incidents in the past where religion and politics have collided in the Islamic world.

One example of the political upheaval concerning Islam is the civil war in Yemen in 1962 in which Saudi Arabia backed the Imam of Yemen (the government) and Egypt backed the rebels. Both sides sent troops into the Yemen and fought against each other based on the version of Islam that they each believed. The fighting escalated and the political situation deteriorated which led to the Egyptian bombing of Saudi towns. However, in the 6-day war in which the Arab countries of the Gulf fought with Israel, Egypt and Saudi Arabia, previously enemies in Yemen were allied in the fight against Israel. Saudi Arabia actually deployed 20,000 troops to Egypt to aid in the fight.

Questions have legitimately been raised as to the validity of the US politically and militarily attacking Afghanistan or Iraq while not attacking another country such as North Korea that has supported terrorism. Specifically, why is the US allied with Saudi Arabia when it is known that the Saudi government has trained, supported and backed terrorists that have attacked US citizens and interests? A brief explanation that follows may answer this question.

The Sunnis in Iraq under Saddam Hussein attacked the Shi'a government in Iran in 1980 and the two countries were at war for 8 years. At the time this suited the US interests in the region. Because of political beliefs, the Sunnis, the Shi'as and the Wahabis are continuously at odds. So why attack Iraq and not Iran or Saudi Arabia? Iraq was weakened after the first Gulf War, the US was able to gain a strong presence in the Persian Gulf. It also projected the GWOT into another area of the world - away from US territory. It also allows the US to have a major presence for the containment of Iran and its nuclear program and terrorist exportation business. Iran is now surrounded by US forces in Iraq, Afghanistan and Uzbekistan. The US has a major presence in the Gulf States of Bahrain, Qatar and the UAE.

The ideal situation for the US in the war on terror, is to have an ally in the Persian Gulf that supports our interests and maintains a close relationship to fight the war on terror. However, this has not been the case. The Saudis have played both sides of the war. They have funded terrorism and allowed al Qaeda to grow and organize. In the May 2004 al Qaeda attacks in Saudi Arabia, several of the terrorists were allowed to escape if they stopped killing their hostages.[18] The Saudis view their use of the Western powers for their benefit as being advantageous, however, the US has a different view and its interests have not been met. The Saudis say they are cracking down on the terrorists, but have funded the terrorists and paid homicide bombers to attack Israel. Although the Saudis tolerate the US, they do not agree with major items in the US foreign policy. For example, after the US was attacked on 9/11, the Saudi Crown Prince visited ground Zero and stated to Mayor Rudy Giuliani that the US must look at its own foreign policy and how it has effected the Palestinian people to understand the reason for the attack. He bluntly stated that the US was at fault for the attack due to its foreign policy.[19]

Saudi Arabia is not a close ally, especially in the war on terror, but is a necessary ally. The idea that we back the Saudi government for access to the Persian Gulf and its trade lanes is only partially true. By maintaining presence in the Persian Gulf, the US foreign policy infuriates the Sunnis and Shi'as, and maintains a division between the governments of the Persian Gulf – the Iranians don't like the Saudi government, the Lebanese don't like the Iranian influence in their country and the Saudi's allowed US forces to base aircraft and personnel in their country which previously infuriated Iraq. It also allows the US to have an influence in the area that no other country can have.

The United Arab Emirates, Qatar, Kuwait and Bahrain have been open to the West, but have not been active politically or militarily to make a major difference individually. The political pressure that the US has heaped upon Saudi Arabia has kept the Gulf States divided in the Islamic realm. It is very important for US interests in the area that the Islamic governments do not become too friendly to each other- hence an Islamic Hegemony. Presently this strategy appears to be working. The point of this discussion is to keep the pressure on Islam in this vital area so there cannot be a unification of Islamic governments in the Persian Gulf.

If the Kingdom of Saudi Arabia falls politically, it will involve outside pressures from nearby countries such as Iran. In their active exportation of the Islamic Revolution, Iran's desire for a Shia-Khomeini style government in Saudi Arabia or Iraq is the ultimate goal. Picture an Islamic theocracy in Saudi Arabia or Iraq that would ally itself with Iran.. This would be the West's second worst case scenario in the Persian Gulf. A nuclear-armed Pan-Islamic Theocracy in the Persian Gulf concerning peace and trade in the Mid-East would be the absolute worst case. As the US turns over sovereignty to Iraq, the IAEA cannot yet verify that Iran has does not have a nuclear weapons program.

Chapter Three
Iran and Terrorism

Iran-al Qaeda Connection (Rise of Islamic Militants)

Astonishingly, most people in the US are ready to believe that al Qaeda is the sole enemy of the US and few other countries or organizations including past enemies such as Iran could be involved in the terrorist attacks on the US. It has occurred to some in the political arena that the terrorists and their sponsors (Iran, Syria, Saudi Arabia) may have something to do with the attacks on America. What is astonishing is the premise that Sunnis and Shi'as are not working together against the US and its interests. Although al Qaeda has been described as an independent terrorist organization with its own organic financing and training regimens, it still has ties to other terrorist organizations and states that sponsor terrorism. The main sponsor and harbinger of al Qaeda is not Saudi Arabia as most think, but Iran. Iran has had ties with al Qaeda since the early 1990s and has been involved in its training and support.[20] [21] [22]

Iran has been known to sponsor Hamas, Hezbollah, Palestinian Islamic Jihad and the Islamic Brotherhood of Gaza in their attacks on Israel. Believing Iran has ties and contacts with other terrorist organizations does not require a large leap of faith. Hezbollah has had the infamous honor of being the terrorist organization that, prior to September 11, 2001, had killed more Americans than any other organization. The attacks on the World trade Center and the Pentagon changed that situation, as al Qaeda became the main terrorist enemy of the US. The potential for two terrorist organizations to merge and organize is very disturbing to peace loving people of the world. The Egyptian Islamic Jihad has already merged with al Qaeda bringing with it a wealth of information and experience.[23] Should Hamas, Hezbollah or the Palestinian Islamic Jihad merge with al Qaeda, the results could be disastrous for the West. However, Hezbollah is making moves to do just that. The common thread linking al Qaeda and Hezbollah is the current Iranian government. The regime has been an outspoken proponent of the destruction of Israel and the US.

Iranian Terrorist Camps

The exporting of the Revolutionary Ideology is accomplished through recruitment, training and then deployment of Islamic Militants abroad. Training consists of political ideology indoctrination, weapons and explosives handling, urban warfare, surveillance and assassination and are taught to terrorist students in the Ali abad garrison at Qom, Hezbollah camp in Varamine, Darwish training center in Ahwaz or in any other dozen training camps throughout Iran. Thousands or perhaps even tens of thousands have been trained at these camps and are sponsored and supported by the Iranian government. The terrorists are then formed into units, both covert and overt, and are assigned to regional headquarters. The Nabi Akram base is situated in Zahedan and its mission is to deploy personnel and carry out missions in Pakistan. The Ansar base in Mashad targets Afghanistan and the central Asian countries such as Uzbekistan, Turkmenistan and Tajikistan. Other forces are deployed to formations of the Army of the Islamic Revolution in different countries and by all appearances are insurgents. The 9th Badr is assigned to Iraq, the 7th Army for Lebanon, the 5th Army for Turkey and the specific country designated armies such as the Bosnia, Africa, and Sudan Armies.[24]

Specific assignments are issued from the directorates of the headquarters of the specific designated units. Additional areas of concerns are Afghanistan, Pakistan, India, Tunisia, Algeria, Egypt, Morocco, the Arabian Peninsula and the republics of the former Soviet Union. [25]

It is clear from the actions of the Islamic Republic Guards Corps (IRGC) or Pasdaran forces, that Iran is involved in terrorist activities. However, the official stance of the Iranian government on terrorism is different than the reality that has been documented in numerous books and articles. In an effort to appear to be a "non-terrorist state" and in an obvious attempt to defer elsewhere the stigma of being part of the "Axis of Evil", the following statement can be found at the website of the Ministry of Foreign Affairs of Iran. It is signed by the President of Iran.

" The Islamic Republic of Iran is an active partner in the global coalition against terrorism and spares no effort for the success of the international community in uprooting terrorism through sustainable, just and non - discriminatory measures. "

H.E. Sayyed Mohammad Khatami
President of The I.R of Iran[26]

The goals of the theocratic government of Iran include consolidation of power in their country and exporting of their doctrine (Islamic Revolution) for the benefit of increased relations with likeminded individuals. Because they believe their type of government is the best and they would like to have others benefit from the same system that they enjoy, the Mullahs of Iran wish to export their beliefs, not only to Shi'a populations around the world, but also to non-Muslim countries such as Israel, Europe and the US. They do this through Hezbollah and Hamas and the IRGC. The main political and military aspect of Iranian foreign policy that affects the citizens of the US is reflected in the following statement by a commander of a special forces unit of the Revolutionary Guard that operates directly under Khameini.

"...the top goal of the Iranian regime is to fight the United States and Israel and to inflict wounds to the economies and to harm other organs of these two allied enemies of Islam and to endanger their system of justice and their sense of security us a necessity as a way for settling political accounts with them".

Ali Akbar Netegh Nouri

Iran and the New Iraq

Iran also does not want to see a democratic Iraq any time in the near future. It is of great importance to the Iranians that the country remains Islamic and preferably theocratic. A government similar to theirs would put the Iranians at ease concerning Iraq. Because they view the new government of Iraq as a US asset or interest, it is fair game for attack in the ongoing jihad against the US. The battle in Iraq will continue as long as the regime that is sponsoring the terror is in power. To win the war in Iraq and eventually the GWOT, the government of Iran must be toppled or changed.

History of the IRGC and al Qaeda

One of the five Islamic Revolutionary Guards Corps (IRGC) branches is the Qods Force or Jerusalem Force. It is also know as the Pasdaran Force. This Iranian special operations unit has been in the business of training, supporting and funding extra-territorial terrorist groups. The IRGC has two missions that it is continuously running. The first mission is to identify, evaluate and destroy any opposition and organized resistance that can lead to insurgency in Iran. The second mission is to identify and train assets in target countries outside the Iranian borders that will help the IRGC export the Islamic Revolution. The IRGC is initiating violent insurgencies in numerous countries with operatives even in the United States. Its main mission is to infiltrate countries that oppose Iran and evaluate the situation for the appropriateness of an insurgency. The ongoing insurgency in Falujah and Najaf are examples of IRGC inspired insurrections. Once these areas are under control of the US and Iraqi forces, the IRGC will initiate another insurgency in another city such as Tikrit, Kirkuk or Karbala.

The IRGC had established training camps in The Sudan in the early 1990s to train terrorist recruits for Hezbollah and Hamas. In these camps the recruits are trained in hit and run guerilla tactics, assassination, roadside ambush, kidnapping, torture, psychological operations and tactical operations involving mines, explosives and hand grenades. The IRGC is responsible for exporting the Islamic Revolution and has found some support in the Shia population in Lebanon. The IRGC has operatives in most countries with a large Islamic population. Their mission is to infiltrate the area and form relationships with rogue elements or extreme groups and offer support.[27] The training camps are tailored to assist the IRGC in its mission by training Afghans, Iraqis, Egyptians, Algerians and Tunisians that fought in the Afghan war as well as supporting the Islamic movements in Chechnya, Turkey and Egypt. [28]

In 1995 and 1996, al Qaeda operatives contacted the Iranian government with an offer to join forces to attack America. Bin laden had met with Iranian officials prior to the bombings of the US embassies in Tanzania and Kenya. The purpose of the meeting was to establish an "anti-US alliance". Usama bin Laden and al Qaeda claimed responsibility for the attacks in Tanzania and Kenya and bear a resemblance to the Hezbollah attacks on the US and French Foreign Legion forces in Lebanon in 1983. al Qaeda established first a tactical relationship with the IRGC linking it directly to

Iran, but then also approached Hezbollah. A second meeting between bin Laden and the operations director of Hezbollah – Imad Mugniyeh- took place to presumably solidify the strategy for the bombings. Ali Mohamed, an operative of al Qaeda, testified that he had arranged security for the meeting. He went on to say that Hezbollah supplied explosives training to al Qaeda and Al-Jihad personnel. The coordination of training and use of explosives are key elements of the attack and appear to have been provided by Iran. The Iranian Ministry of Intelligence and Security may have provided direct support to al Qaeda in these bombings. Phone records obtained by US officials in the investigation of the bombings, revealed that about 1 in 10 calls from cell phone used by Usama bin Laden and his staff were made to Iran. In the aftermath of the embassy bombings and as a follow-up to the al Qaeda-Hezbollah union, Hezbollah's chief of operations appears to have been promoted to "coordinator" between Hezbollah, Hamas Palestinian Jihad, and its sponsor - Iran. [29]

The relationship between al Qaeda and Hezbollah has deepened with the arrival of Salah Hajir (an alias) a senior bin Laden operative who met with not only with Hezbollah leaders but also leaders from a radical Sunni terrorist organization called Usbat al-ansar. Based out of the Ein al-Hilweh refugee camp in southern Lebanon, most of the terrorists fought in Afghanistan, Bosnia, Kashmir and Chechnya. [30]

The training camps in the Sudan were closed for a time, but may have been reopened. An ongoing relationship based on common interests (training and deploying Islamic Militants in terrorist operations) between Iran and Sudan appears to be expanding. The Sudanese Foreign Minister visited Iran in October 2003 and met with the Iranian Vice President and the Minister of Defense and Armed Forces Logistics Chief. The Vice President of Iran stated that cooperation between the two countries would benefit Islam, while the Minister stated, "unipolarism which toes the line of the Zionist minority has targeted its attacks toward the world of Islam".

Obviously referring to the US invasion of Afghanistan and Iraq, he called for greater defense and security cooperation between the two countries (Iran and Sudan). [31]

Iran and 9/11/2001

Did Iran have ties to al Qaeda before the 9/11 attacks on the World Trade Center and the Pentagon? The answer is yes. While some find this hard to believe, it is a reality. Rohan Gunarhatna, a noted expert on the terror group al Qaeda and Usama bin Laden has documented in his book Inside al Qaeda, that Iran had been working with al Qaeda in terrorist training camps in the Sudan along with members of Hezbollah and Hamas.[32]

In an article published by ABC news (online) - *New Friends, New Ties, Is Iran supporting al Qaeda?*, May 22, 2003, Gunarhatna gives specifics. "Iran has been a supporter of al Qaeda from 1993 to 1996, during which time al Qaeda was based in Sudan," said Gunarhatna. "The Iranian security services [IRGC] and the MOIS [Ministry of Information and Security] supported a number of terrorist camps during the period al Qaeda was in Khartoum."[33]

Hamid Rreza Zakeri was reportedly a member of the IRGC and MOIS. An Iranian official stated that he was expelled from these organizations for "suspicious behavior and connections". A second Iranian official stated that Zakeri was "spying, being an agent and scheming against Islam and the revolution in coordination with Zionists and world arrogance".[34]

In an interview conducted February 18, 2003 with the Al-Sharq al-Awsat newspaper and posted on Worldnet 28 February 2003, the former IRCG officer Zakeri stated that Iran had long ties with al Qaeda. Specifically, Ayman Al-Zawaheri, a senior officer in al Qaeda has close ties with the IRGC Qods Force. This IRGC force has been the organization responsible for exporting the Islamic Militant training and support to terrorist groups including al Qaeda. The IRGC has had joint terrorist operations with Imad Mughniyah who was behind bombings of US civilian and military personnel. The IRGC had a part in training the terrorists and providing planning for the 1983 bombing of the US Marine barracks in Lebanon. Mughniyah has become what amounts to a liaison officer between Zawahiri (bin Laden's second in command) in al Qaeda and the IRGC in Iran. It is believed that Zawahiri is still in Iran assisting al Qaeda members regroup and reorganize with the Iranian government's help. [35]

The former IRGC officer Zakeri stated in the interview that he had no prior knowledge of the attacks of September 11, 2001, but did say that there were models of the World Trade Center, the Pentagon and the CIA building in Langley in the IRGC headquarters building in Tehran, Iran. Mughniyeh apparently approached the IRGC in Tehran and brought a message from al-Zawaheri stating that al Qaeda needed help to carry out an "extremely serious operation in the great Satan's country..." [36]

In October 2003, Fox News reported correctly that al Qaeda members were present in Iran. Because of a sharp divide on authority in Iran, President Khatami stated that the government does not support al Qaeda. However, the Guardian Counsel Mullahs control the IRGC and the Qods force that are suspected of aiding the al Qaeda terrorists.[37] They have not denounced al Qaeda or its attacks on Israel or the US.

Michael Ledeen reports on July 19, 2004 that 384 al Qaeda terrorists including 18 senior leaders are in Iran and living near the Caspian Sea in Chalous and Lavizian. These two cities are very important to the IRGC and the Iranian nuclear program. The facility in Chalus is allegedly an underground nuclear facility and the Shiyan Technical Research Facility is located in Lavizan. One of the largest IRGC bases is located there. It is obvious to those concerned that the IRGC is supporting, hiding and training al Qaeda terrorists in Iran. [38]

In the 9/11 Commission report, it has stated that the al Qaeda terrorists that were involved in the attacks on the US transited through Iran before traveling to the US. The Khatami secular government may not have known about the al Qaeda members in his country, but the Mullahs on the Guardian Counsel most certainly knew. The IRGC is controlled by the Mullahs and the IRGC has had years of contact with al Qaeda in training camps and terrorist events. The report stated that the terrorists were allowed to pass through the Iranian country without having their passports stamped. It is well known that the IRGC has used stolen and forged documents and passports for its operatives. This may include the al Qaeda terrorists as well.[39]

Goals of the Islamic Militants

The Global War on Terror is truly a global war and the enemies of the US are many. The major threats to the US are North Korea, Iran and its terrorist allies Hezbollah, Hamas and Islamic Jihad, al Qaeda and other Islamic Militants (Ansar al Islam, etc) that support a Pan-Islamic State at the expense of the non-Muslim countries. A pan-Islamic State, in the eyes of the Islamic Militants, means the entire World.

While not all of these organizations are a direct threat to the US, many of them are a threat in one way or another. Hezbollah, Hamas, Islamic Jihad, Ansar Islam and al Qaeda have all been found to be fighting organizations in the jihad against the US and Israel. al Qaeda is the largest group to strike the US and Usama bin Laden was responsible for the attacks on the US. This group has been able, with help of others, to attack the US and inflict casualties such that the US has not seen before. The attacks of September 11, 2001 will be a turning point, not just for the US, but also for the terrorist organizations and state sponsors that assisted the hijackers.

Usama Bin Laden formed al Qaeda with several goals in mind. One highly prioritized goal is removing western powers from the Islamic Holy Land. Another is the destruction of Israel and the Great Satan (the US). One of the most important goals to bin Laden's plan is the destabilization and fall of Saudi Arabia's Wahabi government and the establishment of a more traditional Islamic government. Also included in the list of goals is the organization and establishment of a Pan-Islamic Caliphate similar to the Caliphates of the past (i.e., religious rulers in Turkey during the time of the Ottoman Empire).

The fall of the Saudi government and the establishment of a new Caliphate in the country that controls Mecca and Media seem to be a combined goal. To achieve these goals, bin Laden must accomplish several lesser goals that include the right of assumption to power based on his interpretation of Islamic law and recognition by other Islamic states of his political/religious power. Once this has been achieved, bin Laden will be able to control a vast portion of the Persian Gulf and the 2/3 of the world's oil reserves. To these ends, his forces of al Qaeda will use every means at their disposal to accomplish these goals.

Chapter Four
Jihad: War or Religious Struggle?

Verse of the Sword

To Westerners, the word *Jihad* has been a word of war on the part of the Muslims. Some interpret it as a Holy war. Many Muslims deny that the word *Jihad* means Holy War and state that the actual Arabic word for war is *harb*, and the word for fighting is *qital*. "Jihad is any action done to further the cause of God".[40] Peace-loving Muslims explain that Jihad is mostly a spiritual battle and is the core of social activism in Islam. Indeed, an important part of the daily life of a Muslim is to strive or "make jihad" to improve society. However, to some, Jihad does mean *war* or at least *fight*.

Many believe it is their obligation to wage Jihad against the enemies of Islam. An enemy of Islam is anyone who has been invited to become Muslim, but declines. Jihad, therefore, is a war against non-Muslims. Motivation for the Jihad comes from passages in the Qur'an and from hadiths. The Islamic Militants have interpreted a specific passage in the Qur'an about Jihad which is called "the Verse of the Sword":

"So when the Sacred Months have passed, then fight the Mushrikin [unbelievers] wherever you find them, and capture them and besiege them, and lie in wait for them in each and every ambush. But if they repent and perform the Salah [Islamic prayers five times daily], and give the Zakah [alms as required by Islamic law], then leave their way free. Verily, Allah is Oft-forgiving, Most Merciful."[41]

A violent military interpretation of the passage could be a rallying cry for the militants' motivation. It may be controversial, but it seems the militants have taken the idea of the Sura and are using it for their cause. The application by Islamic Militants of Sura 9:5 is found in this statement by Ibn Kathir (1301-1372)

"Do not wait until you find them. Rather seek and besiege them in their areas and forts, gather intelligence about them in the various roads and fairways so that what is made wide looks even smaller to them. This way, they will have no choice, but to die or embrace Islam." [42]

Is this the ultimate goal of the Islamic Militants? To kill the enemy or convert them to Islam? Possibly. To some of the Militants, this is the root of their cause. This and several other ideas appear to motivate Islamic militants to fight non-Muslims.

A defensive jihad was also described as reason to fight by Muhammad. A jihad in the defense of Islamic land and defense of the Ummah (Islamic community) was also a reason to physically fight and destroy the infidels. The Crusades (1095-1270) were an example of a defensive jihad. The sultan Saladin was able to effectively rally a force of Muslim fighters presumably in a jihad to oust the Christian invaders. Usama Bin Laden has stated unequivocally that one reason for jihad against the US and its Western Allies is the occupation of Arab lands.

"As for the United States, I tell it and its people these few words: I swear by the Almighty God who raised the heavens without pillars that neither the United States nor he who lives in the United States will enjoy security before we can see it as a reality in Palestine and before all infidel armies leave the land of Mohammed, may God's peace and blessing be upon him". Usama bin Laden [43]

The Rise of Militant Islam and al Qaeda

Two of the most important events in the rise of militant Islam in the last 50 years have been the Iranian Revolution of 1979 and the Soviet-Afghan war (1979 to 1991). The Iranian revolution transformed Iran socially, politically and economically. Shah Palavi's regime was overthrown by the Islamic militants and instigated by Ayatollah Khomeini, an exiled religious leader. Identifying the US as the "Great Satan", the US embassy was captured and US personnel were taken prisoner. The idea behind the Embassy takeover was to stop the US from trying to derail the revolution. The US had, in the past, assisted the Shah in putting down other rebellions (1953 and 1963).[44] Once in power, the Ayatollah's revolutionary party initiated changes in the country and implemented a foreign policy that emphasizes:

Vehement anti-US and anti-Israel Stances;

31

Eliminating outside influence in the region;

Exporting the Islamic Revolution;

Support for Muslim political movements abroad[45]

Iran, in the past twenty years, has become a major player in State sponsored terrorism. Dozens of terrorist training camps exist, well supplied by the government in support of exporting the Islamic Revolution. Thousands of Islamic Militants have been trained at these camps. The Jihad declared by the Ayatollah Khomeini in 1979 is still active today. Iran backs terrorist groups such as Hezbollah, Hamas, the Palestinian Islamic Jihad, the Popular Front for the Liberation of Palestine-General Command and all groups opposed to the Arab-Israeli peace process.[46]

The second notable event was the invasion of Afghanistan by the Soviet Union in 1979. The war against the Soviets was fought by the Afghani's initially and then Muslims from around the world joined in to protect the Ummah. For 10 years the Islamic militants fought the Soviets and eventually witnessed the withdrawal of their enemy from Kabul. Usama bin Laden was a key player in the fighting, financing and organization of the Mujihadeen during that time and gained much respect and many followers. Afghanistan had, in practice, become a proving ground for the Islamic militants. Once the Soviets were defeated, the militants eventually dispersed, but directed their attention toward the US (Beirut 1982-87, Persian Gulf 1991, Somalia 1993, and Philippines 1989-? And now Iraq 2003).

"Jihad, bullets and martyrdom operations are the only way to destroy the degradation and disbelief which have spread in the Muslim lands." (al Qaeda recruitment video) [47]

Usama Bin Laden was a veteran of the war with the Soviets in Afghanistan and viewed by the Islamic militants as a leader for their cause. al Qaeda was established to bring together Arabs who fought in Afghanistan against the Soviet Union." A deeply religious Muslim, he and Sheik Dr Abdullah Azam began formulating and articulating the master plan of the jihad. It was Azzam, not bin Laden that conceptualized a global network of fighters which would one day become al Qaeda. [48]

Finally arriving in Afghanistan after organizing forces in the Sudan and Pakistan, bin Laden and Azzam began working on increasing the size and effectiveness of al Qaeda. The newly formed organization had inherited a full-fledged training and operational infrastructure funded by the US and Western allies during the war with the Soviets. He continued to recruit new fighters from the vast database he had of Mujihadeen. Azzam was murdered in 1989 under mysterious circumstances and bin Laden took control of al Qaeda.

The organization remained untouched until about 1993, when the Egyptian and Saudi governments became aware of al Qaeda and disrupted the organization in those countries, but al Qaeda was strong enough by that time to survive. Being in Afghanistan allied with the Taliban government that provided sanctuary and support, al Qaeda grew.

Between 1993 and 1996, the IRGC provided support for the terrorist organization and structured the logistics and the curriculum. The curriculum itself deals with direct-action terrorism homicide attacks, improvised explosive device, forgery, and assassination. In al Qaeda's case, the operatives went one step further and have managed to establish independent funding operations to support their cause in the West. Credit card fraud is a major source of income with which al Qaeda has been successful, especially in Europe.[49]

Through the direction action of Usama bin Laden, al Qaeda began supporting campaigns against "false" or corrupt Muslim rulers (Saudi Arabia, Egypt, Uzbekistan) and assisting Muslims victimized by non-Muslim regimes (Phillipines, Kashmir, Bosnia, Chechnya). In February 1998 Usama bin Laden issued the statement under the banner of "The World Islamic Front for Jihad against the Jews and Crusaders" stating that it was the duty of all Muslims to kill US citizens – civilian or military – and their allies everywhere.[50] Because he considered the US a "paper tiger", he thought that the war with the US would be easier than the war with the Soviets. He had apparently thought the Soviet Union was the stronger of the two super powers.

The goals of al Qaeda appear to be the destruction of "the Jews and Crusaders". Destruction of the Western powers and Israel is the primary goal. The current goal of al Qaeda is to establish a pan-Arabic/pan-Islamic Caliphate throughout the world by working with allied extremist groups to overthrow regimes it deems "non-Islamic" and expelling westerners and non-Muslims from Muslim countries.[51]

Islamic Militants and the Jihad against America

During the First Gulf War, the Islamic Militants took offense to the deployment of American and Coalition troops on Arab soil. After the war, the US maintained several training camps and bases from which to deploy troops should the need arise. Usama bin Laden and others in the area stated that this was an attack on the Islamic world and the US was humiliating one billion Muslims. Using this as a rallying point, several attacks were launched not only at the US, but also at its allies. Specifically, the Saudi Government was targeted due to the belief by the militants that the Saudis were consorting with the Western non-Islamic powers. This, they said, brought great shame on the Islamic world and they were infidels for doing so and had betrayed the Islamic faith. Several attacks targeting Saudi officials and foreign workers were launched, some of them successful. The Saudis identified elements of al Qaeda as the primary suspects. They responded by arresting suspect terrorists and supporters, which outraged the militants. These attacks continue with mostly westerners being targeted.

Late in 1992 the militants attacked the Gold Minor Hotel in Aden, Yemen in which 100 US soldiers were staying prior to deploying to Somalia. On February 26, 1993, Islamic Militants bombed the World Trade Center causing damage, killing 6 and injuring dozens.[52] US troops in Somalia in October 1993 engaged thousands of al Qaeda members, Islamic Militants and local militia from warlords in the area. An 18-hour battle in the capital city of Mogadishu occurred with hundreds of casualties suffered by the Islamic Militants. Eighteen US Soldiers were killed and over one hundred were wounded. [53] On June 25, 1996, the Militants attacked the US base at Al-Khobar Towers in Dharan, Saudi Arabia, killing 19 US Servicemen and wounding dozens more. On Augusts 7, 1998 the US Embassies in Kenya and Tanzania were attacked with vehicle bombs. Hundreds were killed in the attack. On October 12, 2000, the USS Cole was severely damaged with loss of life as a result of a maritime vehicle attack. September 11, 2001, the World Trade Center was destroyed and the Pentagon was damaged in the infamous attack.[54]

The militants have been striking at soft or unprotected targets, which will cause a tremendous psychological effect as well as material destruction. Militants have attempted on several occasions to assassinate the leaders of the US, Egypt, the Phillipines [55]Afghanistan and Pakistan. Other attacks include attempted destruction of aircraft with various types of bombs and surface to air missile attacks. These violent and destructive terrorist-style attacks, some of them not in an Islamic land, have been used by the Islamic militants as a type of jihad against the US.

The book **Onward Muslim Soldiers**, *How Jihad still threatens America and the West* by Robert Spencer (2003) explains in detail the openly violent contempt that the radical Muslims have for Western freedoms and tolerance based on Islamic documents and statements. Yashiya Emerick's work **Understanding Islam**, (2002) explains the peaceful intentions and lifestyle of Islam and understanding the powerful teachings of Muhammad and the Qur'an.

Is Jihad social activism or a holy war? Emerick states that Muslims must be active in the social affairs of any community they live in. Being active in the society has many aspects. The economic, political, or religious activities of an individual define his or her character. In the United States, the political system is separated from the religious system and therefore, political activities do not usually coincide with religious. However, in most of the world, *political and religious identities are bound into one system.* For many Muslims, being active in society in a political sense is also being active in a religious sense. Followers of Islam recognize a key phrase from the Qur'an which states that Muslims must "encourage good while forbidding evil". Islam is a proactive way of life, meaning Muslims are taught to get involved and take action in the defense and search for the truth.[56]

The generally accepted definition of a holy war is an armed conflict dedicated to religion. A second meaning of war is to strive or contend. Emerick defines Jihad as "to struggle or strive". A Muslim that is active in social events and struggles or strives to change the political and religious atmosphere is involved in Jihad.

However, social activism is not war. Peace-loving Muslims can be socially active in any country and not be involved in what the Western countries define as a 'holy war'. Islamic militants seem to have taken the next step in escalating their own Jihad by making war on the West -- specifically the United States. From the text of the Qur'an, one cannot say that it promotes violence. The people that interpret the Qur'an or hadith in a violent manner, coupled with their own violent beliefs, appear to be involved in Islamic militant activities. In **Onward Muslim Soldiers**, Spencer cites several passages in which Muslims and Muslim clerics rally others behind their own violent beliefs.

"Get out your weapons," commanded Jaffar Umar Thalib, a forty year old Muslim Cleric, over Indonesian radio in May 2002. "Fight against [Christians in Indonesia] to the last drop of blood". Spencer goes on to state, "Jaffar not only incited his followers to violence but gave that violence the legitimacy of Islamic doctrine."[57]

The idea of a pan-Islamic State is not a new one. The Ottoman Empire ruled the area of Turkey, the Middle East, the Balkans, Serbia, Bulgaria, Hungary, parts of Austria, North Africa, Spain. The last Caliphate was abolished in 1924 when Kemal Ataturk founded the Republic of Turkey.[58]

The ultimate goal of a pan-Islamic state, according to the Muslim Brotherhood of Gaza (a forerunner of Hezbollah, Hamas and Islamic Jihad), requires a spiritual phenomenon of an "Islamic reawakening".[59] This would ideally occur throughout the world. Once the Islamic reawakening occurs, the establishment of an Islamic political power as the Caliphate would occur.

Usama bin Laden believes in the pan-Islamic State with a Caliphate (spiritual religious leader) and is using all means at his disposal to accomplish that goal. Bin laden and al Qaeda have been working to overthrow "non-Islamic" governments and expelling Westerners and non-Muslims from Islamic countries.[60] Although al Qaeda is not the only enemy of the US, it is one of the most organized and potent terrorist organizations in the world

Chapter Five
Iran: Nuclear Power Rising

In 1968, Iran signed the Nuclear Non-proliferation Treaty as a non-nuclear state. During this time, it was known that the Shah of Iran was beginning a nuclear energy program for civilian use. There was also a nuclear weapons program that paralleled the civilian program until the Islamic Revolution overthrew the Shah in 1979. After consolidating power in the years after the Revolution, Iran was attacked by Iraq and the war cost both sides significant casualties and resources. In 1984 Iran chose to start its nuclear program in earnest in response to the threats in the region. It was a slow process until Russia agreed to assist the Iranians in rebuilding the unfinished and war-damaged Bushehr nuclear plant in 1989.

Nuclear program

From the beginning, Iran stated that the nuclear program was for civilian energy use and not for a weapons program. However, due to the volatile nature of the region and the potential for military conflict, in addition to countries in the region pursuing nuclear weapons, Iran has been suspected of running a covert nuclear weapon program.

Since 1979, Iran and the US have been at odds on many levels including the nuclear program. However, limited Human intelligence assets have been developed in Iran that can effectively monitor the nuclear program. The exception to this is a group called the National Council of Resistance of Iran (NCRI) which is the political offshoot of the Mujihadeen e Khalq (MEK). This group has individuals on the ground and have reported on many instances of troop movements, government reorganization and suspected nuclear sites. However, the MEK and the NCRI have been outlawed by the US and placed on the List of Terror Organizations. The reasons are political and involve the 'appeasement' ideology of the EU and the idea that the US can gain favor from the Iranian Mullahs by outlawing the MEK and NCRI.

Until October 2002, the Iranian government denied having an active nuclear weapons program. Due to the agreements with Russia and the ongoing construction and rehabilitation of the Bushehr nuclear plant, Iran claimed that their program was for peaceful purposes. The NCRI reported on several areas of suspected secret nuclear facilities in Iran that were not disclosed to the IAEA. The secret nuclear uranium enrichment plant in Natanz was a significant discovery as well as the light and heavy water reactors in Arak were reported by the MEK and NCRI to the US and UN before either had any intelligence on the new facilities.[61]

Although some enrichment of the uranium is required for civilian reactors, further enrichment can be used in a uranium-based nuclear weapon. To enrich the uranium, centrifuges are used to refine the uranium ore into a usable fissile material. The Iranians had disclosed that their centrifuges were manufactured in Iran but had not disclosed that they received material from other countries. Testing of the centrifuges by the IAEA inspectors revealed traces of weapons grade uranium in the centrifuges. Confronted with this evidence, Iran stated that the material must have come from the centrifuges that were imported, confirming suspicions that Iran was either importing nuclear technology illegally or obtaining it on the black market. [62]The centrifuges have a similar design as the centrifuges initially used in the Pakistani nuclear program. [63] The IAEA found traces of enriched uranium on centrifuges used in Libya. The centrifuges and concentrations of uranium appear to be similar to the Pakistani made centrifuges found in Iran. [64]

In an article from Arms Control Today, Brenda Schaffer stated that in a speech President Khatami declared that Iran was mining uranium form its mines and that uranium enrichment facilities were to be constructed for the civilian nuclear program. A uranium conversion facility is to be constructed in Isfahan in which uranium yellow cake is refined into uranium oxide, uranium hexaflouride and uranium metal. Uranium metal is a dual-purpose technology and has only a few civilian uses. Khatami also stated that Tehran will in the future control the entire nuclear fuel cycle of the Bushehr Light Water Rector. He went on to say that Iran would further develop its indigenous ability to fuel the reactor(s) and that the spent fuel provided by Russia would not be a factor as Iran has decided to control the entire nuclear fuel cycle. [65]

This declaration leads many to believe that Iran does have a covert weapons program and that they are preparing to "go it alone" with its nuclear fuel cycle. The IAEA, through its inspections, has not been able to rule out the possibility that Iran does have a weapons program. Inspection and verification of dual use technology, coupled with the fact that Iran has not been completely forthcoming with its truthful disclosure of its nuclear program, leads many to believe that Iran is close to producing weapons in an ongoing nuclear weapons program.

Iran and the IAEA

The IAEA, the US and the European Union are all very interested in finding the truth about the Iranian nuclear program. Closer cooperation has ensued and has been unprecedented in the efforts of those involved to slow or stop the Iranian nuclear program.

The International Atomic Energy Agency is the world's nuclear watchdog and was established in 1957 within the United Nations. Its mission is to provide safety and security, research science and technology and provide safeguards and verification of member states and implementation of strategic plans to regulate nuclear power. The IAEA has the appropriate status and support of member nations to investigate any alleged misuse of nuclear power specifically the promulgation of nuclear components through unrecognized avenues and also countries that are specifically trying to gather or manufacture nuclear weapons.

Several IAEA resolutions have chastised Iran for its unwillingness to come forward with information on the program and have called on Tehran to sign additional protocols and explain the inconsistencies of its previous disclosures. On June 18, 2004, the latest resolution on Iran was issued from the 35-member board on nuclear safeguards in Iran. The resolution *"deplores*...the fact that Iran's cooperation has not been as full, timely and proactive as it should have been..." It also states, "that with the passage of time, it is becoming ever more important that Iran work proactively to enable the Agency to gain full understanding of Iran's enrichment programme by providing all relevant information..."[66]

On that day the Director General of the IAEA in a press statement said that there were 2 points of contention with respect to previous investigations. One was the question of the 36% enriched uranium. He stated they are "puzzled" by the finding and would like more information. The second contention is that of the P2 centrifuges. The specific questions are "how much was that [P2 a part of the] R&D program" or was it a "cooperational" venture in that Iran is now claiming the centrifuges that had "contamination" of enriched uranium were procured rather than manufactured. It also was mentioned in the press release, that Iran is not reporting its information in writing and misunderstandings have developed.[67]

Germany, Russia and the UK all became increasingly involved when their diplomats called on Iran to come clean with their program and intentions or further support for their civilian program would be withdrawn. Russia, Japan and the EU also postponed and withdrew significant trade options with Iran until the situation is resolved.

Although the IAEA is an international organization and formalities must be followed, it is clear that they are not being aggressive enough with Iran. Just the fact that Iran is responding to the IAEA's inquiries vocally and not in writing leads many to believe the Iranians are lying. An answer to the question, "…from where did the centrifuges come and why was their weapons-grade enriched uranium found in them?" is needed. If the Iranians can't answer those questions in writing with documentation to back their statements, then it is reasonable to believe they are lying. There is no choice for the US and the rest of the world to believe that the Iranians are using the nuclear technology for anything other than a weapons program.

Reasons for Iran acquiring Nuclear Weapons
Reason 1: Blackmail (Release the prisoners or we will detonate…)

It must be remembered that the civilian nuclear program and a nuclear weapons program are two different areas of contention. While the dual use technology is available, the components themselves are not inherently dangerous when certain precautions are taken.

However, a nuclear weapons program is dangerous in and of itself specifically due to the nature of the weapon. If the threat of nuclear weapons production exists, it is dangerous to the region politically. It is assumed that the Iranian government has control of the nuclear program. However, the IRGC is under the direction of the mullahs, and it is that section of the government that is in control of the nuclear energy facilities[68] and possibly the covert weapons program. If this is the case, the Khatami secular government does not have control of Iran's nuclear facilities and only the Mullahs of the Guardian Counsel and their leader Ayatollah Ali Hoseini Khameini have the power over the nuclear weapons. Because the Mullahs control the authoritative power in Iran, it along with the IRGC organization have been called a "state within a state". Some believe that the Mullahs may not have enough control over the IRGC and there are suggestions of rogue operations within the Iranian government.[69] Units of the IRGC may even go "rogue" when a bomb is developed. The aggressive nature of the IRGC and the hatred of the US and Israel is evident in their training and political indoctrination. It is possible that the IRGC either under orders from the Guardian Counsel or on their own may launch a nuclear attack on Israel, Iraq or the US. The IRGC is a main political and military force of the Mullahs regime and is a key element and force to be reckoned with in the New Cold War.

The commanding officer of the IRGC has stated in the past that a Cold War has already begun in terms of political confrontation in the Persian Gulf region – specifically Iran. Yahya Rahim Safavi in a speech to IRGC officers in the city of Qom in April 1998 stated

" Can we withstand America's threats and domineering attitude with a policy of Détente? Can we foil dangers coming from America through dialogue of civilizations? Will we be able to protect the Islamic Republic from international Zionism by signing conventions banning the proliferation of chemical and nuclear weapons[70]

A rogue nation with nuclear weapons such as Iran that can wield the threat of nuclear destruction over the region is very dangerous. Depending on the section of the government or the military/political unit that does control the weapons, threats and extortion of the weaker nations of the Gulf is possible. A rogue IRGC fanatical element with nuclear weapons is tantamount to absolute insanity as the use of the weapon(s) would most definitely be destruction of the IRGC's - not necessarily the Khatami government-- enemies. This includes Israel, the Gulf Cooperation Counsel Members – Kuwait, UAE, Bahrain, Qatar and Oman – as well as the US itself.

Even more terrifying is the idea that Iran would allow its terror associates to have access to a nuclear device. A rhetorical comment prefaced with an unreasonable demand by the terrorists would be all they need to detonate a nuclear device. A simple statement such as " Release our Mujahideen from captivity or you will experience the total destruction of the Islamic bomb…" may be the only warning of an impending nuclear detonation.

Reason 2: Deterrent

As we have seen in the past year or so, the Iranian government has had to "come clean" in exposing its covert nuclear program. With the weapon of mass destruction and terror, Iran is well on its way to breaking through "détente" that Commander Yahya Rahim Safavi spoke of. In his mind, the US and Iran are already in a New Cold War *and his statement was made in 1998*. It appears that Iran is trying to follow a strategy of deterrence by assured mutual destruction in its Cold War confrontation, while reserving a first strike capability.

Whether the threat of destruction to Iran is real or not, the Iranian government and especially the IRGC feel that it is. The implication, in the speech by Commander Safavi, that Iran should withdraw from the international treaties concerning nuclear weapons and chemical weapons is most dangerous to the world community. Withdrawing from the NPT will put Iran on the fast tract to joining the nuclear weapon club with devastating international side effects. With the ownership of a nuclear weapon, the responsibility to safeguard the weapon is paramount. When Iran develops a nuclear weapon it will probably be under the guise of defense and the need to counter Israeli nuclear power. However, if Iran does not demonstrate its ability to control its nuclear proliferation, i.e. becomes a nuclear supplier to terrorist organizations; the US and world community will have to step in to control the situation.

For what purpose would Iran use the weapons? It appears that according to former President Rafsanjani that the first use would not be intimidation, but would be used to destroy Israel.[71] Although on the surface that seems to be the initial use, other hypotheses must be explored. The Iranian nuclear weapon can be used as a region force deterrent; a political ace concerning international embargoes, etc; or it can be used to destroy Iran's enemies. Once its use has been defined, the intent of the Iranian government to follow through with its threats must be evaluated. This will establish the parameters in which the Iranians wish to confront the US and its allies – the rules of the New Cold War. The subsequent weapons developed would be evaluated for the intended use within those rules, i.e. the threat of a nuclear detonation is not a threat unless the intent of the Iranians to follow through with the threat is real. Evaluating the political history of the Mullahs, it seems that they would detonate a nuclear device if it appeared to be in the best interest of Iran's political future. However, detonating a nuclear device against a perceived enemy without provocation will be the beginning of the end for the Khameini government.

The idea that Iran needs a nuclear weapon program to defend itself from Israel and the US is a thinly veiled disguise at attempting to acquire nuclear weapons for consolidation of region power. Iran is a more likely target of Israel due to its expanded nuclear program which threatens the US, Israel and the region.[72]

Reason 3: Prestige (nuclear club - Iran will be taken seriously)

Along those lines, Iran feels that it needs to be taken seriously in international affairs. Currently, there appears to be no political contribution that the Iranian government can supply to the international community except the abandonment of both state-sponsored terrorism and its quest for nuclear power. Iran can offer no services or support to bolster the UN, or other international organizations. It simply views the UN as a forum for its own use in which it makes its political views well known. The Mullahs government is a taker - not a giver.

Contrary to Iran's centrist ideology, the US, the EU, South Asia, Australia, and Russia are just some of the nations that give to the international community to make the world a safer place. Iran is one of the reasons the world is not a safe place and continues to play both sides of the international divide as it strives for nuclear power. Because the Iranian government has no apparent redeeming qualities in the international community, it feels that by acquiring nuclear weapons, it will be taken seriously.

However, given Iran's past record on violations of human rights, the propensity for violence and the blatant attempts to export the Islamic revolution through terrorism, attaining membership in the nuclear weapons club may be the end of the Khomeini style government. The government of the Islamic Republic may want to re-think its goal of attaining nuclear weapons. Without demonstrating responsibility in controlling its nuclear programs, Iran's membership in the nuclear weapons club will be viewed by the other members as an intolerable act of self-importance. When Iran feels it is not being taken seriously, they will detonate a nuclear device somewhere in the Mid-East. or they will allow their terror associates to acquire a device and detonate it in Israel or the New Iraq. At which time they will become an insufferable danger to the world and will face their own demise.

Reason 4: Economic

Iran's need for an exclusively peaceful nuclear program is based on the idea that, although Iran is an oil rich country with large reserves of oil and natural gas, Iran cannot rely solely on fossil fuels. Specific points include:

-Continued use of energy in its present form is bound to turn Iran into a net importer of crude oil...

-Local use of these resources as fuel will drastically affect Iran's foreign exchange earnings from export of crude oil and natural gas.

-Iran has vast gas reserves (World's second largest reserves)[73] But their development is extremely costly and the costs can only be offset by gas export as envisaged and implemented in current gas development projects.

-In the projected 7000 megawatt scenario, Iran will save 70 million barrels of crude oil annually with an economic value of $1.5 billion annually.[74] The argument continues to escalates the tension between the US and Iran by stating the following:

The advisability of a nuclear energy program for Iran was even endorsed by the US State Department, which in a memo of 20 October 1978, [before the Islamic Revolution] stated that the US was encouraged by Iran's efforts to expand its non-oil energy base, and was hopeful that the US-Iran Nuclear Energy Agreement would be concluded soon and that American companies would be able to play a role in Iran's nuclear energy projects

The assertion now that Iran, because of its gas and oil reserves and resources does not need nuclear energy can not be sustained. This assertion is clearly based on the state of relations rather than concern about non-proliferation. [75]

Iran's government states that it invokes its 'inalienable right' to pursue nuclear power and further cites the IAEA's Article II of its Statute that states: "The Agency shall seek to accelerate and enlarge the contribution of atomic energy to peace, health and prosperity throughout the world". [76]

The opinion of the Iranian government is that it is seeking an alternate fuel source and that it has been following precedents set in the past by other countries (Israel) and the IAEA statute applies to all countries.

However, the pursuit of nuclear power in a country that is militant by nature and radical by definition, is worth monitoring. This is the same government that states it is 'an active partner in the global coalition against terrorism', (see above) yet has multiple terrorist training sites and is known and documented to have supported and sponsored terrorism against US and Israeli interests. The IAEA and the UN have a duty to the world community to monitor the pursuit of nuclear power of any country, especially one with a view of exporting revolution. However, monitoring of nations is not a monopoly and the technologically advanced countries with the capability also have a duty to the world to monitor countries with the desire to develop nuclear power. This includes the US, The EU, Russia, Japan, Australia and other countries with concern. Strict control of dual use technology is imperative.

Impact on the region

Speculation on the impact of Iranian nuclear weapons will have on the region is difficult at best. There are dozens of scenarios and an infinite number of possibilities in which there would be a US and Iranian confrontation. However, the scenario that the US will face in the Mid-east with Iran is one of Mullah hardline conservative Islam. The Mullahs will continue to tighten their hold on Iran and consolidate their power.

49

To do this, they will either have to rebuild their conventional forces to the point of economic/military equilibrium or develop unconventional weapons such as nuclear and chemical weapons to "defend" themselves from threats both inside and out. Currently, it appears Iran believes it is cheaper to build a nuclear arsenal with an indigenous fuel cycle than to rebuild its conventional forces.

While most countries in the world will react politically to a nuclear-armed Iran and condemn the acquisition of nuclear weapons, some countries will perceive a very real threat to their sovereignty. Countries such as Turkey, Saudi Arabia, Egypt may see the Iranian nuclear buildup as a threat. This, in turn, would lead to a nuclear proliferation in the region spurred by fear of nuclear attack from Iran. Should this happen, nuclear non-proliferation would be in danger of being hijacked. States in the region that perceive a threat to their borders would be jumping on the nuclear bandwagon and a second nuclear arms race would ensue.

As we have become more aggressive in fighting the Global War on Terror, the various facets of the war have begun to surface. These facets include the quick victories in Afghanistan and Iraq, but also the battle against the insurgencies in both countries. Nuclear proliferation and the New Cold War are also facets of the Global War on Terror. If the world does not come together on the issue of preventing nuclear proliferation, the existence of the NPT and the UN/IAEA will be in jeopardy. While the corrupt and impotent UN continuously demonstrates its ineptitude at solving international problems, it still is an international forum for debate and concern. The IAEA is for the most part, the only nuclear watch group that can get the answers to the questions pertaining to nuclear proliferation.

In any case, the proliferation in the Gulf is dependent on the actions of Iran and its foreign policy once it does develop a nuclear weapon with a delivery system that could reach Israel, Western Europe or Central Asia.

50

It is apparent that if the world community allows Iran to develop nuclear weapons, it will cause severe political instability in the Persian Gulf Region. Given the current political situation in Iraq and the Persian Gulf, along with the proliferation of nuclear weapons, countries in the region will escalate their nuclear and conventional forces to the point the area will erupt in violence. If nuclear weapons are used in the conflict, hundreds of millions will die and the world will be plunged into further chaos in the aftermath of a nuclear catastrophe.

Chapter Six
Science and nuclear weapons

Nuclear technology

At this point it is important to understand the basic mechanics of a civilian nuclear program and its potential for a dual role as developing material for nuclear weapons. In a civilian nuclear power facility, electricity is generated from the heat of uranium fission to create steam to drive a conventional turbine power plant. There are several types of reactors that can use different levels of fissionable fuel. Facilities and plants are needed to prepare and enrich the uranium. Once the fuel is used in the reactor, the process yields depleted uranium, metal and ceramic fuels and also spent and irradiated fuel. A reprocessing of the different types of fuel can separate the depleted uranium from the remaining enriched uranium and radioactive wastes. Some of these wastes can be used in military applications.

One of the problems with separating civilian and military applications is that both share the same processes of enrichment and the materials to do so. A byproduct of enriched uranium is plutonium, which is now being used in mixed-oxide fuel reactors. The plutonium can also be used as a material component in a nuclear warhead. Nuclear capable countries assisting non-nuclear capable countries with nuclear reactors and technology increases the possibility of nuclear material and other technologies proliferating in the 'non-nuclear world'. Indeed, after becoming established, these countries have begun trading with each other in nuclear materials, technicians and technology.[77]

Iran's Scientists working at the Tehran Nuclear Research Center (TNRC) at the University of Tehran are actively working on laser enrichment, plutonium reprocessing and weapon design research and development [78]

Inspections and disclosures by the NCRI and the Iranian government have revealed that the nuclear program is much further along than previously suspected especially with the discovery of the uranium enrichment facility at Natanz and the heavy water reactor at Araz. Iran appears to have developed three avenues for obtaining fissile material and producing nuclear weapons. The fissile material needed can be procured from

1. The Light Water Reactor from Bushehr,
2. The Heavy Water Reactor at Arak, and
3. The capability of mining uranium ore at Yadz and refining it at the Natanz facility.

While the first two options would yield a plutonium-based weapon, significant infractions of the NPT would be exposed, i.e. diverting material from the civilian program to a weapons program. The third option allows for the development of uranium based weapons system in an essentially covert operation. With the declaration by President Khatami that Iran will be monitoring its own nuclear fuel cycle, Option 1 seems to be the most quickest route to the production of Nuclear weapons. For a long term program that is covert, option 3 is appropriate.[79]

Nuclear weapons

There are two types of nuclear warheads, the atomic fission or the hydrogen fusion. The process of detonation is not complicated, but obtaining the components and detonating them in a proper sequence can be complicated.

The atomic bomb that is composed on fissile material and uses plutonium 239 and uranium 235 achieves detonation by compressing a mass of material that can be split at the atomic level. Two methods of compressing the material are implosion or simultaneous firing of a gun type detonator. This action will allow the material to reach critical mass and release a huge burst of energy in the form of initial blast (overpressure) and thermal radiation (heat). Depending on the amount and type of material as well as the location of the burst, the detonation and resulting explosion can be massive [80]

The combination of fission and fusion reactions are the basis for the thermonuclear bomb. The thermonuclear bomb is similar to the non-complicated uranium based fission weapon but with another stage in the detonation process. Fission splits atoms and as this occurs, heat and energy are released. Additional neutrons are also released to accelerate the cascading process. The fusion of smaller lighter nuclei into heavier atoms also releases energy, but is difficult to achieve except at high temperature and pressure. The above description creates these conditions for a sequenced fusion event. The fusion stage of the thermonuclear bomb involves cylindrical blankets of fusion fuel (lithium isotope) encased in an outer blanket of depleted uranium. Once the initial detonation occurs, the fissionable material releases energy, heat and neutrons that initiate the fusion process which, in a cascading (irreversible) event, cause a massive explosion. The fission-fusion-fission processes increase the effectiveness of the force of the explosion. [81]

Foreign aid and Iranian Nuclear program

Russia has been a partner with Iran in regards to its nuclear research and development program. After years of trying to find a supplier for the Iranian's first nuclear power plant, Russia stepped in and a contract was signed in January 1995 to finish the plant at Bushehr. The $800 million contract calls for Russia to complete the work on the damaged reactors at Bushehr on reactor one in the first four years. In April 2002, Alexander Kudryavtsev, the Russian Atomic Energy Minister stated that the cooperation between Iran and Russia will continue and 5000 tons of material have been shipped to Bushehr. That same month, it was reported that the construction of the main component of the 1,000 MW nuclear power plant was complete. At that time Russia stated that despite US pressure, the reactor will be operational in 2003. However, it appears that Russia is over optimistic and the reactor is not yet operational. Further statements by the Russians have been made and the reactor is expected to be operational in 2005.[82]

Iranian technicians are being trained in Russia at the NIKIET Institute are acquiring knowledge that can be used not only for Iran's Civilian nuclear program, but also for its military program as well.[83] The *Intelligence Newsletter* reported in January 2002, that there were 300 Iranian nuclear experts being trained in various parts of the world with most being trained in Russia. According to the ITAR-TASS news agency Russia is training 600 Iranian nuclear experts and expects that the reactor in Bushehr that is to be manned by these experts to be operational by 2006.[84]

In Esfahan at the Nuclear Technology Center, a Chinese supplied 27-Kilowatt thermal miniature neutron source reactor has been used. Its purpose is to produce isotopes and burns enriched uranium fuel. Iran had, in the past, planned to build a uranium hexafluoride conversion plant at the Nuclear Technology Center with the help of the Chinese. In 1995, there were 15 Chinese nuclear experts at the site who were likely making design preparations for the facility. China is also supplying Tehran with a plant to produce zirconium tubes that are used in the reactor's core. China has also been supplying Iran with data on chemical separation technology that is necessary to consolidate the heavy elements such as uranium and plutonium.[85]

Pakistan and Iran's Nuclear Program

No other episode of proliferation of nuclear weapons has sparked so much controversy than the deliberate transfer of nuclear technology and knowledge by Abdul Kadeer Khan to several rogue nations including North Korea, Iran and Libya over a period of years.

Khan is the father of the nuclear bomb in Pakistan and was hailed as a hero for being able to develop the technology that would allow the Pakistani government to counter its rival and enemy -- India. India and Pakistan are at odds over the area of Kashmir and have had border disputes and on several occasions have gone to war. Pakistan leveled the playing field when it developed its nuclear weapon capability. Apparently, according to Dr Khan himself, there was no transfer of hardware, just designs.[86]

One of the pieces of information transferred was the centrifuge design. It is estimated that Dr Khan and eleven scientists working with him made hundreds of millions of dollars selling the information. There is suspicion that the Pakistani government was involved, but this has been denied by President Musharref. The proliferation controversy has had a demoralizing effect on the country and the implications that Dr. Khan may be responsible for accelerating the nuclear weapons programs of Iran, North Korea and Libya are shocking.[87]

The Black Market and nuclear components

As early as 1994, the black market was a good source of nuclear technology, parts and associated technology. Dual use technology and parts are the largest sector of the black market trading. Most of the smuggling is coming from Eastern Europe through Poland to the West and then sold on the market to the highest bidder. Material such as uranium is being smuggled for a price of $700,000 per kilo. Russian security forces have stopped several attempts at smuggling, and in one case over 80 kilos of uranium were recovered (equivalent to $56 million). There has been a growing fear that radioactive material from active and inactive facilities in the former Soviet Republics of Kazakhstan and Uzbekistan are being smuggled out of Central Asia and may end up in the hands of Islamic Militants. Couriers were stopped in Moscow, St Petersburg and Volgograd.[88]

The smuggling is dangerous to the extent that there is direct involvement of rogue nations in obtaining nuclear material and technology on the black market. The potential danger is for a rogue nation or terrorist group to assemble a nuclear device. However, the smugglers are also suffering from overexposure of radiation while they have the material in their possession.

Libya has admitted to obtaining nuclear technology and material on the black market with the intent of enriching uranium. Libya has recently given up on its nuclear weapon program and has turned over material and bomb making plans to the US. At a Department of Energy facility in Oak Ridge, Tennessee, the material and technology is being investigated and cataloged. It appears that Libya has in the past had arranged to purchase 10,000 centrifuges to enrich uranium. If the fissionable material had been available, Libya would have been able to produce "several" bombs *per year*. If Libya has been able to obtain this kind of technology with virtually no detection, then Iran could be as equally clandestine in its methods to obtain the same equipment and technology.

Russia and Iran's Nuclear Program

The Russians seem to be taking a big brother approach as far as the nuclear dilemma is concerned. They want to supply material for the nuclear program, monitor the fuel source and then dispose of it so the Iranians cannot use it for a weapons development program. One problem with this is that Iran has its own uranium mines and can use that material to develop a weapon in a parallel program. China and North Korea have participated in Iran's nuclear program. The North Koreans do not want participate in talks with US unless it can benefit from the talks. It has been evident that North Korea wants to use its nuclear arsenal for blackmailing the US and in a last ditch effort use them on invading US troops. The IAEA has tried to monitor all these countries and their ties with Iran, however, the methods are not foolproof, and there is no ongoing minute by minute intelligence gathering mission to stop Iran from starting up its nuclear facilities.

Therefore its seems to be logical that it is only a matter of time before the nuclear facility in Bushehr is on line (2005) and if the Natanz facility is capable of converting the enriched uranium into plutonium, then there will be several types of nuclear weapons.

The other fuel source of weapons is uranium itself, but it must be enriched. The IAEA has found residual enriched uranium in equipment in Iran. On June 26, 2004, Fox news has reported that Iran will pursue its uranium enrichment program using large numbers of centrifuges. Pakistan itself has tried to help other countries develop nuclear programs. Dr. Khan has specifically assisted Iran, Libya and now it is reported on the Fox news channel and the LA times that Syria was also a country that was given technology and knowledge of nuclear weapons. The design and application of centrifuges are similar the ones used in Pakistan.

The problem with all this is, that with the rogue states and nuclear proliferation, there has become quite a bit of black market activity centering around former Cold War enemies such as Russia and Poland.

There appears to be a black market pipeline through Poland that transports nuclear/radioactive material that is being smuggled out of Khazakstan which may ultimately find its way to Iran or other countries or organizations (al Qaeda) that are pursuing nuclear capability.

Several large finds have been uncovered in Poland that were being smuggled. There are several dangerous problems with this activity. First being that the material can be used for nuclear weapons, the second is health of surrounding populace – the material is being smuggled *unprotected*. The smugglers are receiving a lethal dose of radioactivity. Also there is no controlled monitoring method that can be applied when exiting these counties. However, some of the former Soviet states are establishing sensors to detect radioactive material at border checkpoints. The material can be shipped or carried around the world in a variety of ways. Unless government authorities are specifically looking for radioactive material –such as the US- this material can go undetected. The black market is a major problem and will be a source of material to rogue states even if a monitoring system is put into effect.

So when Iran states that it will now control its own nuclear fuel cycle, along with the declaration that it will continue its uranium enrichment via centrifuges purchased on the Black Market and the vow that it will use nuclear weapons on Israel, one would think that Iran has a strong nuclear weapons program in place.

The key to an Iranian controlled nuclear fuel cycle is its ability to obtain the uranium and enrich it and refine it to use in the nuclear energy program. The following is a diagram of the nuclear fuel cycle with the addition of nuclear fuel from Russia and the possibility of diverting the enriched uranium/plutonium for weapons development.

The Nuclear Fuel Cycle

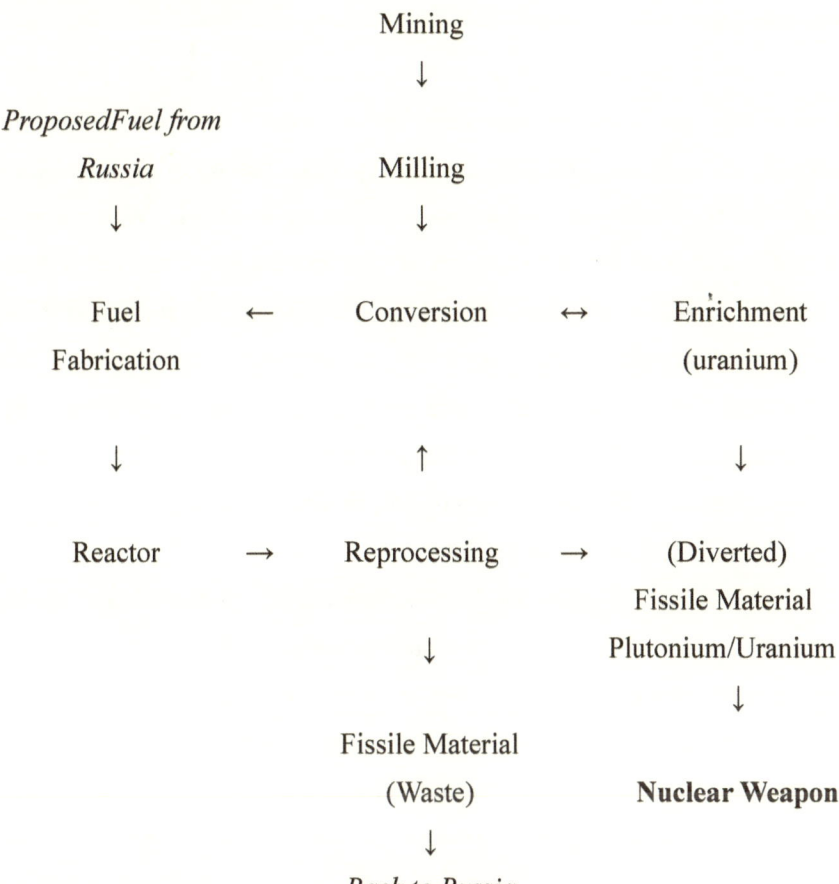

Nuclear fuel cycle and Iran's resources

Uranium is the key element used in nuclear fuel for nuclear reactors. It is *mined* from the ground in either open cast pits of by underground mining. This can be completed at the uranium mines in Yadz. Then it is refined or *milled* in Yadz. Then it is consolidated into fuel in a *conversion* process and this would take place in Isfahan. This uranium is then *enriched* so it will produce more energy. There are several places that this can occur such as Karaj, Sharif, TNRC and Natanz. This is the point in the process that uses the centrifuges to enrich the uranium. If it is enriched to a higher quality, it can be used directly in nuclear weapons without any further refinement.

At this point the fuel is *fabricated* into the fuel that the particular reactor can use. Iran has four light water reactors in Bushehr that are coming on line soon. There is also a heavy water reactor at Arak that Iran neglected to disclose until it was discovered by the MEK. Yadz, Sharif, Bushehr and Araz can be the sites of fuel fabrication. The fuel is then used in a nuclear power *reactor* to heat water to steam and turn the turbine to produce electricity. The reactors in Bushehr and Araz are two of the reactors that can use the fuel. There are also other non-energy producing research reactors that can use the fuel as well. These are located in Tehran Nuclear Research Center, the Bonab Atomic Energy Research Center, and the Isfahan Nuclear Research Center.

When the fuel is expended, it is *reprocessed* into plutonium and can be used in the reactor for power or in a nuclear weapon. This can take place in the Tehran Nuclear Research Center. At this point in the process, in the case of Iran, the nuclear waste would be transported back to Russia. However the Iranians have stated that they are going to develop their fuel cycle and not rely on outside assistance. If the fuel cycle is completely indigenous (does not have to be returned to Russia), the reprocessed plutonium would then be *diverted* for use in a nuclear weapon.

Both uranium and plutonium can be used in a nuclear bomb. The bomb that was used against Hiroshima in WWII was a uranium-based weapon and the bomb used on Nagasaki was a plutonium-based weapon.

Methods of deploying nukes

Nuclear weapons can be made in many sizes and shapes with a variety of detonating devices. Delivery can be as simple as detonating the device where it is built or as complicated as mounting it on a cruise missile and sending it thousands of miles to the target. Most countries that have nuclear weapon capability launch the weapons via ballistic missile, air drop delivery system or cruise missile. However, the nuclear device can be delivered via ground transportation as well as by boat. Because of its massive destructive power, the weapon can be detonated near the target and still destroy it.

This type of weapon in the hands of terrorists can be devastating. It is difficult to track and if, for instance, a cargo ship carrying a nuclear device pulled into the harbor in Los Angeles, the resulting explosion would no doubt destroy much of the area and damage an area far beyond. Delivery of the weapon can be in as many forms as one can imagine. Currently nuclear devices are delivered via missile, artillery shell, man-pack portable 'suitcase' bombs and vehicle mounted delivery.

Missiles

Iran possesses the most missiles of any country in the Persian Gulf region with a capability of producing and improving the range and payload. Not only can Iran develop and produce new missiles; it has imported modern ballistic missiles from North Korea and China.

The missiles Iran purchased from China are the CSS-8 model and have a range of approximately 150km. Although it is a short-range missile, it can reach Baghdad from Iranian territory. The Scud missile has a range of 500 km. Used extensively in the first Gulf War, missiles rained on Israel and Coalition forces with unpredictable results. The North Korean Nodong 1 has been modified by the Iranians who renamed it the Shahab 3 and tested at least once. It has a range of 1300 kms and can reach Israel from Iran.

These missiles can be loaded with chemical, biological, nuclear or conventional warheads. The larger the warhead, the smaller the payload. As the expertise of the Iranians increases with help from the North Koreans and the Chinese, the range and payload of the weapons will increase.[89]

In WWII, Nazi Germany developed the V-1 (rocket) and the V-2 (unguided missile) to exact vengeance on the UK, hence the 'V' for vengeance. While essentially unguided, these weapons wreaked havoc on

London and the English countryside. The V2 was substantially larger than the V-1, but the mission was the same - as much destruction as possible. Those weapons were loaded with conventional warheads. Many of the V-2 rockets targeted not only British cities, but also cities such as Amsterdam. Had the Nazis had the motivation to use chemical or biological weapons, (which it had) the casualties would have been much worse. The Iranians are creating their version of the vengeance weapon.

The Chinese and North Koreans are currently working on more advance missiles to deliver larger multi-use payload system. The Shahab 4 is speculated to be a version of the North Korean Taepo-Dong 1 rocket that is a three-stage space launch vehicle. This looks to be the modern version of Iran's vengeance weapon. This missile appears to have the capability to reach Western Europe. It has a 2000km range and 1000kg payload [90]

The Taepo-Dong 2 missile that North Korea is currently developing could be used by the Iranians. With modifications and a lighter payload in a three-stage configuration, experts agree that the missile could reach the US. It is estimated that this missile could be tested within the decade and as seen by other tests of missiles by the Iranians, it would be considered operational.[91]

To summarize, Iran has a current and ongoing nuclear program that may or may not involve nuclear weapons. Concurrently, it is developing its inter -continental ballistic missile technology so that it can launch a missile with a potential nuclear payload to, first, Western Europe and then, to the continental US by 2010. [92]

Cruise Missiles

A much better use of resources and technology suggest that a cruise missile is more economically feasible for a country like Iran. With limited resources and an ailing economy, spending large amounts of cash to acquire missile technology just doesn't make as much sense as developing a cruise missile. There are more military applications for a cruise missile as far as deployment of chemical or biological weapons. A cruise missile flying in a straight or even circuitous route could deploy a large amount of the special weapons to a more specific target area. Although weather and wind conditions need to be taken into account, the ability of the cruise missile versus a ballistic missile to deploy weapons aver a specific target area is more appropriate to a terror state such as Iran.

The cruise missiles can also be loaded with a nuclear weapon. Although the cruise missile has a shorter range than a ballistic missile such as the Shahab-3, it can be more effective by flying in low under radar and other air defenses. In addition, a combination attack of ballistic missiles and cruise missiles would be more effective, possibly overwhelming the target country's air defenses. Along with its military application a cruise missile could be used as a terror weapon by being used to "randomly" attack enemy targets at the edge of the target countries air defenses. Cruise missiles currently in use or acquired from foreign sources include: HY-C-201, Harpoon, HY-2 Silkworm, AS-9 and AS-11 cruise missiles. Effective range is from 50-120kms with a payload of 130-513kg.[93]

Aircraft Launched Nuclear Weapons

Simple methods to utilize organic aircraft assets include employment of ground and fighter attack aircraft, which includes Su-24s, MiG-29s, F-4D/E and F-14A. Iran has had much trouble in keeping the air assets mechanically operational. Lack of spare parts for US aircraft resulting from sanctions imposed by the US has hindered the Iranian Air Force. However, limited trade and supply of aircraft parts from Russia have kept a hand full of Soviet Built aircraft flying. The target countries such as Israel and Turkey have an extensive air defense system that would be able to target aircraft entering the danger zone. This method of delivery is probably the least effective means of delivery and is not applicable to targets except in the immediate region.[94]

Artillery/Rocket Launchers

Artillery rounds and technology have come a long way from the WWII massive artillery bombardments. Modern warfare employs artillery rocket systems and Iran has the Oghab artillery pieces that can launch nuclear devices approximately 45 kms. The Nazeat artillery rockets can reach 120km with a 150kg payload. [95]

Nuclear Component Smuggling

Another method of deploying nuclear weapons to the target is to smuggle components into the target country. While this is controversial, it is not as difficult as some might think. A journalist smuggled a radioactive material into the US through the port of LA without being detected in 2003. For the anniversary of the September 11 attacks, ABC News in 2002 assigned correspondent Brian Ross to carry depleted uranium from Austria to Istanbul. The authorities did not discover the depleted uranium and he was not detained in any of the countries.

The depleted uranium was then shipped to the US and into New York.[96] Graham Allison, a former assistant secretary of defense, stated: "What indeed is the most likely way that a nuclear weapon would be delivered by a terrorist to the US?...The most likely way is in a cargo ship".[97]

In a May 9, 2004 article in the Los Angeles Times by Douglas Frantz, "Threat of 'Dirty Bomb' Growing, Officials Say", the cesium, strontium and cobalt found in long abandoned Soviet nuclear facilities can be used in a 'Dirty Bomb'. A dirty bomb consists of three components: a large package of conventional explosive, a detonator and a proportionate amount of radioactive material wrapped around the conventional explosive. When it is detonated, it causes an explosion that spews radioactive material in all directions in a dynamic radius.

Once the components have been collected at the target site, the nuclear device (dirty bomb, uranium-based or plutonium based nuclear device) could be transported to the target or detonated in place. Currently, the US

Homeland Security has radiation detection devices roaming major cities to detect such weapons or components of weapons. The instruments are so sensitive; it can detect radioactive material used to medically "tag" blood during cardio-stress tests. Although the material is radioactive, it dissipates from the body over a period of days. Several persons, according to news reports, have been approached asking if they were recently involved in such medical tests. The roaming units had apparently detected the radioactive material while the patient had been driving on a major freeway. Should one of these radiation scanners be present at the major ports, it is likely that true radioactive material (depleted uranium is depleted of most radioactive material) will be detected and stopped enroute to the target area.

Associated Press reported in an article dated May 06, 2004, that in Kiev, Ukraine, 375 pounds of cesium-137 (radioactive material) was seized from three men from a city in the Crimean Peninsula in the Black Sea.[98] This amount of radioactive material could be used in a dirty bomb. The material could easily be transported out of the country through a port in the Crimea to almost anywhere in the world.

Another frightening consideration is that Iran is preparing to strike the US with terror attacks that would include any weapon from its arsenal. This includes chemical weapons, as well as the conventional terror weapons such as car bombs, etc. In June 2004, two Iranian intelligence officers, identified by the FBI as IRGC officers, were caught video taping potential terror targets in New York City.[99] They were subsequently expelled, but it was the third episode they were found videotaping targets. A foreign affairs analyst for Fox News on June 29, 2004, stated that the Iranians were evaluating targets to attack in America should the US or Israel attack or attempt to destroy Iran's nuclear program. Their mode of attacks could be as simple as a homicide bomber or as complicated as a smuggled nuclear device-- possibly a suitcase nuke.

Manpack Portable City Busters

The governments of Central Asia have had nuclear weapons in their countries in the past decades when the Soviets had stationed the weapons there. The Soviets are gone and most of the weapons are gone as well. Presumed to have been in the custody of the Soviets, there may be as many as 100 "suitcase" nuclear bombs that are missing from the Soviet arsenal.

These weapons are small man-pack nuclear devices that can be detonated by a small group and al Qaeda has boasted that it already has several of these devices in its hands. The danger from these bombs is relevant to the target or target system that the enemy is trying to destroy. One bomb is devastating, but several bombs detonated in different parts of a major city or in several cities could be disastrous. The main problem for the West is to find these weapons and confiscate them. Unfortunately, the suitcase bombs are probably not in Central Asia anymore. Finding and stopping the enemy from using the weapons is a difficult process, and their appeal is that they are easily concealed. However, they do contain radioactive components that could be detected with radiation monitoring devices. Having the "suitcase nukes" is one thing, but moving them into place is another.

Iran has already stated that the international situation between Iran and the US is going to come to a military confrontation and have devised nuclear strategy to destroy the US when it invades Iran. Several aspects of this policy are very self- damaging as the Iranian strategy uses nuclear weapons on its own soil which will no doubt kill hundreds of thousands of civilians to get at the US troops.

Except for the Shahab-4 missile, Iran currently is capable of all the above. Whether they choose to use one method or a combination of methods, it appears the Mullahs are striving for missile dominance in the region.

Nuclear Detonation

"The discovery of nuclear chain reactions need not bring about the destruction of mankind any more than did the discovery of matches. We only must do everything in our power to safeguard against its abuse."

Albert Einstein

A nuclear detonation is the most destruction man made force. The initial blast can heat surrounding air to tens of millions of degrees[100] and as it cools rises developing into the horrific mushroom cloud with which we have become familiar. The explosion transfers energy into the blast, thermal radiation and nuclear radiation.

The blast of the explosion causes most of the damage to the target area and consists of the shock wave, ground shock, water shock, cratering and dust and radioactive fallout. Thermal radiation –extreme heat -causes destruction with electromagnetic, infrared, ultraviolet light and x-rays at the time of explosion. The gamma radiation and neutrons that are emitted from the explosion are emitted within the first minute.[101]

The transfer of energy or how effective the explosion will be is dependent on location of detonation and weather conditions. Detonations are characterized by their location which include sub-surface burst, surface burst, and air burst. A sub-surface burst will not cause as much as a problem because the ground or water absorbs the energy. Other hazards caused by this type of explosion include cratering and ground or water shock. This is the least effective method for surface destruction.

A surface burst is one that is detonated on the surface or slightly above it. The transfer of energy is most effective if the fireball appears above the ground. Devastation is concentrated at ground zero with destruction of the over-pressure of the blast wave and transfer of thermal energy which results in large and very hot fires. The residual radioactive particles from dust and debris that is spewed into the atmosphere result in fallout and is a danger.

An airburst which is an explosion in which the fireball does not reach the surface and causes considerable damage due to the unobstructed shock wave and thermal radiation. Burns to skin and eyes along with injury and damage from the blast and thermal damage which involves the subsequent destruction from fire are extensive. The electromagnetic pulse and ionizing radiation will destroy or damage communications, computers and satellite to ground links.[102]

There are varying sizes of nuclear weapons. The bomb used on Hiroshima, 'Little Boy'was approximately 13 Kilotons (one ton equals energy release of 1,000 of TNT[103]) and 'Fat Man' was approximately 20kt and destroyed Nagasaki.[104] Today members of the nuclear club have in their arsenal bombs ranging from a few kilotons to 53 Megatons. While in the past, the superpowers developed weapons that would destroy entire cities with one blast in the range of 10megatons (MT), most nuclear weapons in the past 10 years have been estimated to be in the 200-500 kiloton range.[105] The reasoning is based on the effect of multiple detonations of medium size weapon being greater or more effective than just one large weapon that has a greater chance of being intercepted.

The Medium Atomic Demolition Munition (MADM) had a yield of 1-15kt and weighed about 400 pounds. It was designed to destroy tunnels, bridges, dams and disrupt enemy troops movements. The W54 Special Atomic Demolition Munition (SADM) weighed approximately 163 pounds and had a yield of up to one kiloton. It was man portable and was stored in a case the size of a suitcase – hence the name – suitcase nuke.

The application of these type of weapons or weapons that have been or are being developed for use against the US by Iran, North Korea or a terrorist organization would probably use a nuke between one and twenty kilotons. The smaller nuclear devices would destroy several city blocks and cause fires and radioactive fallout with a limited EMP. The effect would be mostly psychological if only one was used. However, the terrorists have used imagination in the past to obtain their goals and would undoubtedly wish to use their few weapons to cause maximum damage. A 20kt detonation will ignite most materials in a 1mile radius depending on weather conditions and the lay of the land. At 2 miles, most people would suffer 2nd degree burns and paper or dry leaves would ignite.[106] There would be a great amount of damage secondary to the fires caused by the thermal radiation. Most analyst and experts agree that a wartime nuclear attack would involve several detonations in relative close proximity and within a short period of time.

One of the most horrific results of conventional bombings was the firestorm and destruction of Dresden. Over 3,300 tons of incendiary bombs were dropped on the city resulting in a firestorm that killed approximately 135,000-150,000 people, over half being children. Over 11 square miles of the city was razed. 3.3 kilotons of explosives were dropped over a period of time. An equivalent detonation of a 3.3 kiloton bomb would no doubt cause more destruction through the over pressure blast but result in a large amount of damage from fire.

If three one-kiloton nuclear devices were detonated in close proximity in an American city, would the results be similar? It is difficult to tell. However, if terrorists ignited incendiary fuel through car bombs near the edge of the destructive radius after the detonation of three small yield nuclear weapons, the results would probably be similar in destruction. Even without the incendiary devices, one or two 15-20kt devices would cause tremendous damage and probably start a firestorm as in Hiroshima and Nagasaki.

On August 11, 2004 Iran test fired the enhanced Shahab-3 missile which was a success.[107] The missile, which was previously successful in a test in 2002, has been enhanced and is claimed to be completely made in Iran. It is based on the North Korean No-Dong missile. It is assumed that the Shahab-3 missile can mount a medium sized nuclear weapon (approximately 1MT) as its payload. With this type of offensive weapon, it would be possible for Iran to launch a weapon and detonate it near Israel and "walk in" several missiles into the country in a series of successive launches. This poses a grave threat to the area

Chapter Seven
Iran's Domestic Plight

Islamic Revolution

The Islamic Revolution of 1979 was a milestone in political science and was as important to modern history as the French Revolution of 1782 or Russian Revolutions of 1917 (Kerensky reform revolution July 1917 and the Bolshevik revolution October 1917). Ayatollah Khomeini's objective was more than just a replacement of the Shah. He was determined to instill a theocratic government based on Islamic law and Sharia. This would purge Iran of pro-western influence and consolidate control through the Mullahs.

Controversially, the marks the first time in modern history that a legitimate government was overthrown for a theocracy. The revolution motivated the people and cultivated the idea that the state's version of Islam was not pure. The Western influence, the foreign presence, the corruption and the strict rule over the country under the Shah provoked many in Iran to look elsewhere for a solution. Ayatollah Chimney, a Shi'a Imam, exiled in Paris was able to return to Iran and unite the people to overthrow the government.

Today, the president of Iran voices the opinion of the government in several statements about the revolution as an ideology rather than an event. "No world power can defeat the Iranian nation thanks to the national resolve and the Islamic faith". [108]President Khatami continued in his speech to the thousands of personnel of the Islamic Revolution Guards Corps (IRGC) stating that the Islamic Revolution shook the political structure of the world. Comparing the politics of the Islamic Republic to that of the "Marxist states" (the Soviet Union and its communist allies) and the "liberal democracy" (the US) he stated that the Marxists have learned their lesson and the "liberal democracy" should have learned that the Islamic Revolution proved that democracy will not work in Iran.

The ideology of the Islamic Revolution is based in the total condemnation of the West's immoral and exploitive role, the influence of Zionism and the Jewish occupation of Palestine and the denunciation of the pro-western Muslim regimes[109] The Islamic Revolutionary Guards Corps (IRGC) is tasked with exporting the ideology and enforcing the Islamic rule in the land. The organization is controlled from the top and answers to the Mullahs. It appears to serve the Islamic republic in a similar manner as the KGB served the Soviet government.

Iran has been undergoing a reform movement since 1997 with the popular election of President Khatami, however, within the hardline government there is real opposition to the reform movement. The hardline theocratic Mullahs that have power in the Iranian government continue to consolidate their power by finding and eliminating opposition. In 1988 30,000 political prisoners were executed after being found to oppose the Khomeini government. Since 1997, the conservative forces have tried to intimidate the reform forces by using public smear campaigns, informal and illegal vigilante groups, in the name of Allah attack reformists on the street. These vigilante death squads have abducted and murdered "close to 100" activists and intellectuals.[110]

In 2004, hundreds were arrested mostly in student demonstrations for "incorrect" political thinking. At least 108 executions were carried out and 197 people were sentenced to be flogged.[111] This action by the hardliners follows a pattern of violence, oppression and outright assassination set down years ago. In March of 2000, a close confidant of the Iranian President (Khatami), Saeed Hajjarian was shot in Tehran. Vigilantes associated with the hardliners have attacked several prominent reformists and the modus operandi of the attackers appears to have been similar as the pro-reformists in Iran blamed the hardliners.[112]

The reformists have recently suffered a major set back as the elections of February 2004 were won almost exclusively by the conservative hardline political leaders. In essence the political reform movement is at a standstill with the Mullahs consolidating their power and eliminating their opposition...all in the name of the Islamic Revolution.

Sharia

The strict system of law that the Islamic republic and other conservative Islamic countries (Syria - Sunni Sharia, Saudi Arabia - Wahabi Sharia) have instilled is based on Koran and Arabic law systems. It also exhibits traces of Bedouin law, commercial law from Mecca, agrarian law from Medina, Roman and even Jewish law.[113]

The sharia law system is practiced in many countries including Saudi Arabia, Sudan, Yemen, and Iran. Until it was destroyed, the Taliban in Afghanistan used the sharia law system and followed it to its extreme. Shooting female Muslims for not properly covering themselves at public executions appeared to be occurring on regular basis. The harsh punishments are the result of the sharia law system and is what most Westerner's feel is so barbaric about the Arab culture. The idea that a hand should be cut off for stealing, or a women is stoned to death for (alleged) adultery are two punishments that have been seen on news reports and highlighted by news magazines. The application of the law and its punishments are varied from region to region.

Daily Life: Unemployment and civil discourse

The state controls most of the infrastructure of the Iranian economy and it is showing signs of instability and major distortions of profit throughout the marketplace. Inflation is relatively high and stands at about 18%. The over reliance on oil production and foreign economic agreements have forced both President Rafsanjani and later President Khatami to enact economic reform with little success. Private business is restricted to services, farming and small-scale workshops.[114]

It appears that although Islam has not lost its appeal to the Iranian people, the Islamic Revolution has. The ideology of the Islamic Revolution as a political doctrine interpreted and enforced by the hardline conservative Mullahs has "lost its flavor". Political factionalism has divided the ruling Mullahs leading to political inconsistencies and contradictions. The government is theocratic rather than autocratic and the religious leaders appear to have consolidated their power and are not willing to share it or lose it. The theocratic government combines all aspects of government and religion together to from a religious government, hence the interpretation and enforcement of religious doctrine. There is no separation of religion and politics.

Physical separation of men and women is a given fact in the daily life of the Iranian people in public places. Social reform is slow in progression because of the hardliners view and harsh enforcement of Islam. The younger generation appears to be finding ways to circumvent this and underground social gatherings are taking place on a more regular basis. Other indulgences include non-traditional music from Europe and the US. The leading conservative cleric in Iran states: Society is on the threshold of an explosion. If popular discontent increases, society and the regime will be threatened". He went on to say, "No regime can maintain itself in power by force".[115]

45 million people in Iran (64%) are under the age of 35. Islamic law strictly regulates the times and places and situations in which young people can socialize. There are dress codes and curfews. Contact between unmarried couples is forbidden. It appears that these strict rules of socializing in public have molded the younger generation of Iranians into "pessimistic, rebellious and arrogant" socialites. According to Amanollah Gharayi Moghadam, a sociology professor in Tehran, much of this behavior is caused by the strict limitation imposed by the 'conservative authorities'. He goes on to say that the younger generation, which makes up 2/3 of the population of Iran is losing touch with Islam and has no interest in politics or tradition. [116]

In late June 2003, over 4,000 protestors were arrested in demonstrations against the hardline clerics. The demonstrations were spurred on by university lecturers, students and writers who called on Khameini to abandon the principle of being God's representative on earth and to accept his accountability to the people.[117] Most protesters have long supported the opposition to Iran's unelected hardline clerics (the Mullahs in the Guardian Counsel) while supporting the popularly elected President Khatami. However, due to his inability to demonstrate any major reform in the Islamic Republic's government, the protestors have denounced Khatami as well. Political analysts have stated that Iran's hardline approach to dealing with the reform movement only makes matters worse and the opposition grow. [118]

Hardliners and Reform - Separation of Mosque and State

History has demonstrated that effective governments that represent the people fairly and promote an environment of trust have separated religion from politics. In Iran's theocratic government most of the control is in the hands of a few - the Guardian Counsel, which is extremely hardline and the conservative Islamic Fundamentalists that believe in the traditional Sharia laws. As stated earlier, the Sharia is derived from the Koran and other historical law establishments in the Middle East.

President Khatami was elected by popular vote replacing Rafsanjani, promising a list of reforms that would lessen the stranglehold by the Mullahs on the populace. However, his plan for liberalizing Iran has been essentially defeated by the Guardian Counsel. Khatami favors an Islamic democracy rather than a complete theocracy. The differences in opinion, however, are moot as the real power of the government belongs to the Guardian Counsel.

Separation of Mosque and State is a concept that would essentially unravel the Iranian theocracy. Sayyid Hussein Khomeini, the Grandson of the Ayatollah Khomeini fled Iran due to the abuses of the 'tyrannical rule'. He is apparently a popular religious figure with the younger generation and has supported the reformists in the past. The hardliners are worried that he will become a symbol and rallying point against the regime and has sent a unit of Revolutionary Guards (IRGC) to search for him. Khomeini has stated, Iran needed "…a democratic regime that does not make use of religion as a means of oppressing people and strangling society". He also has stated that there is a need to separate mosque and state and expects the movement opposing the Iranian regime will gain momentum.[119]

The effect of separating mosque and state will have a very damaging effect on the Mullahs and their hold on absolute power. While they have intentionally intertwined religious laws with social laws and traditions, separating them will cause the Mullahs to lose legitimacy. Redefining or changing laws, or even having two sets of enforceable laws, will prove to be difficult for the Guardian Counsel in that the people expect a fair system. The social reform movement is a popular one and the oppression caused by the strict religious codes will cause the Guardian Counsel to redefine itself before it redefines the socio-legal infrastructure.

Chapter Eight
US – Iran Foreign Policy and Relations

Modern Political History of Iran

The political historical background of the nation that affects the world today is a story of Old World Persia meeting the internationally new Iran.

Until the 1920's, the country was known as Persia and had a distinct and violent history. Prior to that time, the culture was based on Islam as it is today, but the political structure was based on rule of a Shah (or King) in a series of dynasties. A traditional way of life was common in small towns and large cities.

In 1921, Reza Khan, an Army officer organized a coup d'etat and set up government naming his dynasty Pahlavi after the ancient language. Through a series of programs he tried to Westernize Iran. He consolidated government control and centralized his authority. He changed the government bureaucracy and administration as well as created an extensive system of primary and secondary schools. In 1935 he established a western style university and expanded the economy. He became popular with the middle class. He was not as popular with the clerics during this time. He was determined to break the power of the religious hierarchy and limit the power of the clerics. Reza initially enjoyed popularity with the people, but after the confrontation between the government and the religious clerics in 1936 in which several dozen people were killed in the shrine of Imam Reza in Mashbad, his popularity declined.

In order to modernize his country, he removed effective power of the Majlis, (Iranian Parliament) censored the press and arrested opponents of the government. His tax policies were hard on landowners and peasants and as a result, by the mid 1930s there was much disapproval with the government. Along with limiting the rights and power of the Iranians he also removed the social privileges of foreigners and relations with the Soviet Union and Great Britain deteriorated. On the eve of the Second World War, Germany was Iran's largest trading partner. In 1941 Muhammed Pahlavi, the son of Riza Pahlavi, came to power and assumed the title of Shah of Iran.

During WWII, the USSR and Britain occupied parts of Iran. There were diplomatic problems between the countries during the war over territory and oil contracts. However, Britain pulled their troops out and their influence in the area decreased. The Soviets tried to keep their troops in the area and attempted to absorb the Iranian area of Azerbaijan. However, with the help of the US, the Soviets were forced to withdraw their troops and the sphere of influence in the area decreased. In 1947, the US signed an agreement with Iran for military aid and military advisors to help train the Iranian army.

The Shah consolidated his power after the war and the country's economy and population grew. Yahiya Emerick, a Muslim writer, describes the three decades of the Shah's rule after WWII as an ambitious plan to modernize Iran. He had a secret police organization, the Savak, that was very large and widespread, which enforced the laws that the Shah decreed. The Savak routinely arrested and tortured people in an effort to quell dissent. In 1952, there was a revolution by the people against the Shah that was apparently successful. According to Emerick, a 'countercoup' was orchestrated by the CIA that restored the Shah to power. There was another period of dissent in 1963 which was crushed, again, with US assistance.[120] The religious clerics and the people apparently did not forget the US participation. During this time, Iran became known on the world trade scene due to the needs of the modern world. Oil became a commodity and the Shah's wealth grew.

In 1979, the people could not tolerate the Shah's regime and the exiled Shi'a cleric, Khomeini, returned to spark the Islamic Revolution and overthrow the Shah. His forces also entered the US embassy and captured American diplomats, military personnel and civilian workers whom they held hostage for 444 days. This aggression against the US was in anticipation of a military response. Interestingly, there had been another take over of the US embassy months before. This was in retrospect, a reconnaissance by the militants to grade the US response to their actions. When nothing recognizable was done by the US in terms of retaliation, the 'students' attacked the US embassy in November 1979 and took 66 US hostages. Fourteen were released and the rest were held until Ronald Reagan took office. The Revolutionary government held the hostages in order to stop the US forces, including the CIA from interfering with the government takeover. Khomeini's Revolutionary government was established and reformed and ruled Iran until his death in 1987 The Shah had left Iran and visited the US for medical treatment of cancer. This action infuriated the Islamic militants even more, confirming their idea that the US supported the Shah to his death. Since then the theocratic republic has ruled its 28 provinces under the Revolutionary Constitution that has codified the Islamic principles of government.

Iran Foreign Policy since 1979

After WWII and before the Islamic Revolution of 1979, Iran had been westernized and was aligning itself with Europe and the US. Since the revolution, the views of the government are completely different. The new government was convinced that the US had been supporting the Shah for decades and was trying to keep him in power to the detriment of the Iranian people. After the success of the revolution in overthrowing the Shah and his ruthless dictatorial government, the revolutionaries became emboldened.

Imposing their ideas of Islam on the populace and the witnessing the forceful removal of an oppressive government cultivated a new view. The Islamic Revolution was a means by which all people could free themselves from oppressive governments. A strong commitment to Islam, they speculated, allows the oppressed to defeat the Great Satan (the United States) and the Lesser Satan (Israel) and their imperialist policies. Some see the Islamic Revolution and Iran as the point of the spear in the forceful liberation movement to free oppressed Muslim countries. The Revolutionary government's foreign policy revolves around this idea and actively exports the ideals of the Islamic militants. Iran is a proud sponsor of international terrorism.[121] The Islamic Revolutionary Guard Corps (IRGC) and the Ministry of Intelligence and Security are actively involved in the planning and execution of terrorist events and support a variety of non-Iranian terrorist groups. Iranian assets beyond their borders include IRGC forces known as Pasdaran forces which actively 'export' the Islamic revolution rhetoric[122]

The Iranians support other Shi'a populations, specifically in Lebanon in an effort to export the revolution and are in favor of destroying Israel and recreating Palestine. Although several leaders of the Lebanon leadership did not think that Iranian revolutionary vision was appropriate for their country, the invasion of Lebanon by Israel in 1982 allowed the Pasdaran to obtain a foothold in that country. The Pasdaran have actively supported the Shi'a Muslims in the area and several terrorist organizations as well.

The Iranian Islamic Revolutionary government continues to be extremely anti-American and anti-Israeli. Earlier in 2004, over 30,000 people were killed in the devastating earthquake in the city of Bam. Hundreds of thousands were injured or without shelter and food. However, the Iranian government did not initially allow US support from the government, and only limited numbers American civilian rescue teams or American sponsored international relief organizations to enter their country. This was seen by the Iranians more of a matter of convenience rather than an opportunity to reestablish a relationship with the US.

Government terror inside Iran continues and according to the NCRI, the horror is escalating. The most notable infringement on human rights was the massacre in 1988 of 30,000 political prisoners which were executed for opposing their government.

As mentioned before, Hamas and Hezbollah are two terrorist organizations that have benefited from the Iranian theocratic state. Hamas emerged in 1987 as a splinter group of the Muslim Brotherhood. Active in both the political arena and terrorist events in and around Israel, its main base is in Gaza. Hamas demands the existence of a Palestinian state and the destruction of Israel. Hezbollah is a radical Shi'a organization dedicated to the fundamentalist rule in Lebanon. It provides training for Palestinian terrorists that target both US and Israeli interests. Ideologically, Hezbollah has its motivations in the Islamic Revolution of 1979.[123]

Both Hezbollah and Hamas are not only active in terrorism, but also assist the Pasdaran forces in recruitment. Once recruited, the future Islamic Militant is sent to Iran to one of several training centers. There is quite a large amount of coordination between the Foreign Ministry and the Intelligence Ministry and the Qods Force (IRGC) to recruit and train Islamic Militants.

However, the official stance on terrorism is different. The following statement can be found at the website of the Ministry of Foreign Affairs of Iran.

" The Islamic Republic of Iran is an active partner in the global coalition against terrorism and spares no effort for the success of the international community in uprooting terrorism through sustainable, just and non - discriminatory measures. "

H.E. Sayyed Mohammad Khatami

President of The Islamic Republic of Iran

http://www.mfa.gov.ir[124]

The goals of the theocratic government of Iran include consolidation of power in their country. Because they believe their type of government is the best and they would like to have other benefit from the same system that they enjoy, the Mullahs of Iran wish to export their beliefs. They do this through Hezbollah and Hamas and the IRGC.

US Strategies to deal with Iran since 1979

In 1963, a political confrontation occurred in Iran between the government of Shah Reza Pahalavi and a Shi'a Cleric - Ayatollah Ruhollah Khomeini. An uprising in the streets followed and the Shah exiled Khomeini and put down the rebellion. This was the beginning of the Islamic Revolution in Iran.[125]

The US had a major presence in Iran since about 1953 with the CIA involvement in the counter-coup that reinstalled Shah Pahlavi as head of Iran. President Eisenhower promised US presence and support to Iran and then to Saudi Arabia. This commitment was followed by Presidents Kennedy, Johnson, Nixon and Ford and continued through the term of President Carter. A "two pillar" strategy for US presence in the Persian Gulf developed based on agreements with Saudi Arabia and Iran. These two countries controlled vast resources of fossil fuels and were in a strategic position in the Persian Gulf to attract the interests of the US while overseeing or denying the area to the Soviet Union.

The Carter Doctrine was introduced *after* the Islamic Revolution and the Khomeini takeover. Initially, Carter set out to change world politics from the status quo specifically because the Soviet Empire was making gains and establishing footholds in areas of US concern. After taking office, Carter vowed to remove the American presence from the Korean Peninsula, reduce US Arms sales, reach an agreement to cut strategic weapons of both the US and the Soviets, and engage the Soviets in discussions that would move the political relationship between the two countries from détente to the next level - appeasement. In June 1978 at a speech at the Navel Academy, President Carter stated that he wanted to "increase our collaboration with the Soviet Union".[126]

While observing events in Iran, President Carter and his staff had reassured the Shah that the US would support him in his efforts to stop the popular uprising. The Shah had confidence in the US to back him and even after he had left Iran, he "remained convinced for weeks that the American government all along had a grand strategy that was simply beyond his ken."[127] In an interview with Parviz Shahnawas, an Iranian freelance journalist, the former French President Valerie Giscard D-Estaing disclosed information concerning the Shah of Iran before he fled his country.

In a meeting in 1978, the leaders of France, Germany the UK and the US met on the French Island of Guadaloupe to discuss the Iran. The former French President Valerie Giscard D-Estaing stated in this interview, '…it was the American President who told us that now it's over and we will not support anymore the Shah, and he was thinking that probably there would be a military regime after the Shah. We were absolutely surprised because what we wanted was a sort of peaceful evolution of the Iranian crisis and certainly some political changes were needed but in any way we didn't think at all the regime would be overthrown at once".[128]

Once Iran was lost, the US interests in the Persian Gulf area were suddenly not as solid as once thought. Carter recognized that the Persian Gulf region was necessary to the US and the modern civilization both in terms of oil and strategic location near the Soviet Union. The failure of the Carter administration to stop the Soviets from expanding their empire forced the President to initiate a containment policy in Iran. This was designed to stop the spread of the Islamic Revolution and deny the Soviets an opportunity to move into the Gulf area and undermine US interests. His top priority was to stop the Soviets from expanding their power base from Afghanistan into Iran. To those ends, he initiated a $40 billion program to train Islamic Fundamentalists in Pakistan and Afghanistan to fight the Soviets and protect the Persian Gulf from the USSR.[129] Usama bin Laden joined the Mujahideen to fight the Soviets.

It appears that this was the beginning of the second Islamic Revolution in that the forces of al Qaeda were assembled for the first time. The Carter Doctrine was put in to action shortly after the success of the Islamic Revolution in Iran. The combination of the Islamic Revolution, the rise of Ayotollah Khomeini as the both the spiritual and political leader of Iran, and the massive infusion of money, weapons and training of the Islamic militants that were of the same mind as Khomeini - remove the foreigners from Islamic lands - were some of the elements that motivated the Islamic militant movement. The US program to train the mujahideen began with Carter ultimately led to the rise of Islamic militants in several countries including Pakistan. With the increased capital and ability to train the Islamic Militants, the Pakistani Intelligence organization recruited, trained and supported the Taliban in Afghanistan. The second Islamic Revolution has had two long lasting effects that the world still feels today; the rise of the Taliban and the concurrent rise of al Qaeda.

During the Iran-Iraq War of 1980-1988, the US and most of its allies opposed the Iranian Regime and backed the Iraqis. It was in the common interest of the West to stay out of the fighting and to allow the Iraqis to fight the Iranians. Since the Revolution, the US has imposed import sanctions on Iran which are designed to stop US goods from finding their way to Iran. Also put into place were export controls on Iranian trade goods including fossil fuels. Except for issues that were to be dealt with in the UN forum, the US and Iran had no political dialogue. Even today, there is no Iranian Diplomatic Mission to the US.

With almost all of the economic, political and social ties severed, the relationship between the US and Iran has grown cold. The non-engagement policy that the administrations since Carter have followed has produced nothing noteworthy in the context of diplomatic affiliation and has been referred to as the "cold-shoulder" policy. There are indirect connections to the Islamic Republic, but they are few and far between. There are few, if any, actual US human intelligence assets on the ground in Iran. It is difficult for the US and its allies to gather information in the country. This lack of intelligence and basic information has allowed Iran to develop its nuclear program. Indeed, the US and the UN were shocked at the advanced level of technology the Iranians have accomplished specifically in regards to the nuclear program.

"Here we suddenly discover that Iran is much further along with a far more robust nuclear weapons development program than anyone said it had," Secretary of State Colin Powell stated on CNNs "Late Edition". He continued, "It shows you how a determined nation that has the intent to develop a nuclear weapon can keep that development process secret from inspectors and outsiders, if they are really determined to do it".[130]

Although, economic sanctions, trade embargoes, export controls, and cold should diplomacy have all been used in the past 20 years, it has not stopped Iran from exporting the Islamic Revolution; increasing its number and quality of long and short range missiles, or developing its nuclear program.

Chapter Nine
Europe and Iran

The countries of Europe have been central to the economic and political life of the United States since the mid-1800s. The European Union (EU) is an organization designed to represent the economic interests of not only the traditionally friendly Western European countries, but also countries from the former Soviet block. In May 2004, the EU admitted several countries from the former Eastern Block and has entertained the idea of inviting countries such as Turkey into the group. This is significant because of the EU ties to the Mid-East and countries such as Saudi Arabia, Iraq and Iran. Despite the mounting evidence of a covert nuclear program, ongoing human rights violations that include political oppression, unlawful detainment and torture, the EU has continued to trade with Iran, albeit at a diminished level.

There is no formal contractual trade agreement between the EU and Iran, however, ongoing negotiations are proceeding through the Iranian Embassy in Brussels. Several years ago, after Khatami was elected president, he stood on a platform of reform and willingness to open Iran to outsiders in the hope that an increase in trade and dialogue would ensue. The European Union jumped at the chance to oblige Khatami and negotiations between the EU and Iran began in December 2002.[131]

The Europeans have a long history in dealing with Mid East countries in terms of trade. Despite the UN sanctions imposed on Iraq, Germany, France and Russia continued to trade and supply Iraq. In 2001-02, Germany led the European countries in trade with Iran. Other countries that trade with Iran on a consistent basis are the UAE, Russia, Italy, South Korea, Japan, France, China, Brazil and the UK.[132] Sanctions were imposed on Iran by the US and its allies after the 1979 Islamic Revolution, but since that time apparently only the US is still imposing sanctions and enforcing its trade embargo on oil exportation. [133]

It appears that when the EU feels it is in its own best interest, it will not support its allies such as the US in its non-engagement policy with Iran. The 'disagreement' between the US and Iran is topic of negotiation with the EU, but the interests of the EU are not contingent on the political alliances with the US. Over the past 5 years, Sweden, Italy, the UK, Netherlands, Norway, Spain all have invested millions of dollars in Iran's energy sector with France leading the way with $1 billion in 1999.[134]

Through 2003, the representatives from Iran and the EU visited each other in order to open dialogue to intensify their relationship. The EU has decided that Iran has too great a potential to ignore in the international market. Apparently President Khatami agrees and has visited at least six of the European countries striving for more trade and dialogue. It appears that Iran is trying to gather support to help in its application for membership in the World Trade Organization. (WTO).

Iran's largest trading partner is the EU and imports to the EU from Iran are 80% fossil fuels. Iran imports a variety of items from the EU which include machinery, power generation plants, mechanical and electrical appliances. On the illegal end of trade, drugs grown and refined in Afghanistan make their way through Iran and illegally into Europe. This has caused the authorities to crack down on Iranian imports. The EU sees the drug problem as a major pivot point in its relations with Iran. Also on the list are Human rights violations which include imprisonment, torture and in some cases, protesters that were arrested died in custody.[135]

The EU has stated that it has a firm stance toward Iran on the issue of human rights, but has "refrained to bring up their names [political prisoners] in public negotiations with Iran". This reluctance of the EU to engage the Iranians on their domestic policy of crushing any opposition to the tyrannical regime speaks volumes of their indifference to the human rights issue.

The other major sticking points to negotiations involve the state-sponsored terrorism and the quest for nuclear power. Iran continues to harbor al Qaeda terrorists and continues to train elements of Hezbollah and Hamas. The IRGC is still exporting Islamic Revolution and training terrorists in camps in Iran.

The nuclear program that Iran has been working on has been shown to have several major infractions that the IAEA is investigating. Secretary of Iran's Supreme National Security Council Hassan Rowhani has met with top EU officials concerning Iran's nuclear program in late 2003 and 2004.[136]

With the concern of nuclear proliferation, the EU has been in talks with the US and stressed the importance of monitoring the nuclear program by initiating an additional protocol for inspection and compliance of their nuclear program. The IAEA chastised Iran for its reluctance to disclose information about its program and then negotiated with Iran to agree to the additional protocols. The political force behind the protocol was actually economic. The EU gave Iran the choice of signing the protocol or suspending negotiations for further trade agreements.

The EU has had a relationship with Iran over the past several years that has increased its wealth and relationship with Iran. Despite US pressure to take a "cold shoulder" non-engagement policy with Iran, the countries of the EU have decided that it is their best interest to deal with a country that does not support human rights and tortures their prisoners, a country that is actively pursuing a nuclear program that could involve a covert weapons program, a country that exports terrorism to the Mid-East and the world through organizations such as Hamas, Hezbollah and Islamic Jihad. These organizations have killed hundreds of people including Americans and Europeans. It is interesting that the EU has turned a blind eye to the rogue nature of Iran and instead concentrating on developing a better working relationship. This has been the difference between the US and the EU in terms of dealing with Iran. It has been argued that an engagement policy could achieve more than a "cold shoulder" policy. Logically that is true. It is reasonable to assume that the more the contact with a country, the more the information will be available. However, Iran has kept its diplomatic doors closed so that it is still difficult to access any important information that can be of use in the political realm.

On the subject of a nuclear Iran, the EU and the US are starting to re-evaluate their individual approaches with good results. The US and the EU through the UN and the IAEA have been able to establish additional protocols that Iran must follow if it is to continue its program. More cooperation is need from Iran and both the EU and the US have agreed on the basics of holding Iran responsible for its actions and inactions (such as not disclosing nuclear facilities at Arak and Natanz). Iran may be a catalyst in the relationship with the EU and the US after a chilly divergence of ideology on the Iraq situation. In the aftermath of the First Cold War, the EU with its inauguration of ten new countries, the EU is emerging as a new superpower. The US and EU share common values and goals and the commonalties between the two powers will greatly enhance any future relationship concerning Iran. The firm stand by the EU on the Iranian nuclear dilemma reflects the sincerity of the comments released in a joint statement at the EU-US summit in Goteborg, Sweden, 14 June 2001, "...Experience has taught us that, when the EU and the US work hand in hand, either bilaterally or multilaterally, we can be an engine for positive global change...".[137]

EU-US Strategy of Disarming Iran

No strategy on the subject of Iran's nuclear program can be effective without the two superpowers agreeing on a common platform and very defined set of goals. Without a platform for agreement, there cannot be a "road map" to the completion of the goals. Because of the very different approaches the two powers have had in reference to Iran, a common position must be defined. It had appeared up until recently, that the EU was content with the fact that Iran was pursuing not only nuclear power, but also an indigenous nuclear fuel cycle. The achievement of this goal by the Iranians would greatly change the face of politics in the Middle East. The power derived from the potential of having or readily developing a nuclear weapon would have a 'dividing' effect on the US and EU if there is no common position.

Recently, the EU has stepped up its insistence that Iran disclose all of its nuclear related issues and supported the IAEA in its decision to chastise Iran for non-disclosure and non-compliance under the non-proliferation treaty. It appears the Europeans are concerned that Iran may be hiding a covert nuclear weapons program just as the US has been charging Iran for several years. However, it was initially the goal of the US to stop the Iranians from achieving nuclear power and also stop the quest for an indigenous nuclear fuel cycle. It appears that the Iranians are much closer to obtaining both goals in the near future.

The common position for the EU and the US now is or should be prevention of a *nuclear weapons program*. To this end, the goal of the two superpowers is to work together to *deter further progress on the weapons program* so much so that the Iranians will give up on the process. Prevention, preemption, interdiction and rollback are all viable options.

Diplomacy is obviously key in this situation and to that end, a policy of engagement, even on a small level can produce incredible gains.

The sanctions that the US has placed on Iran have international repercussions in that US allies or associated countries do not want to be in a position of disfavor with the US. The embargo pertains to Iran's oil and its ability to export it on the world market. While Iran is able to export some of its oil to countries around the world, if the sanctions were lifted, it would ease tension in the Gulf. The EU has more than enough economic power in the area as well, so the combination of the two would be potent weapons in the dismantling of the Iranian nuclear program. Concessions may have to be made in the engagement process to get the Iranians to bow to international pressure. Although this would appear to be a reward for *not* pursuing a nuclear weapons program, it would be, in effect, the first step in dismantling not only the nuclear program, but also the strict control of the Mullahs government.

This would add fuel to Khatami's reform movement in allowing more business adventures in the EU and the easing of tensions in reference to the trade embargo. While the hardline government does not wish to pursue a dialogue with the US, most Iranian people do. It is in this context that the US may wish to open a limited indirect dialogue with the Iranians so that the people see the possibility of a new future.

The Iranian strategy of trying to divide the US and EU with diplomatic overtures can be just as effective if the tables are turned. If the US opens a dialogue with the Khatami reformist movement and eases tension from the trade sanctions, Khatami would undoubtedly gain support of the people. Social tension and need for reform is so volatile at this point the Mullahs will lose control eventually. Despotic regimes will fall due to their own inability to change with the popular voice. Diplomatic pressure from the outside can motivate the people to change their government. The combination of the EU and US working from a common platform with reachable waypoints in the roadmap can achieve their goals of dismantling the Iranian nuclear program and bringing down the Mullahs of the Guardian Counsel and possibly ending the New Cold War.

Chapter Ten
The New Cold War

In the context of world events and international relations, the development of a nuclear program by Iran with the intent of obtaining the ability to readily produce a nuclear weapon is contemptible. It compares to the USSR after WWII trying to obtain the nuclear secrets from the US. The results of that intelligence coup resulted in the Cold War. In retrospect, the Cold War is defined as starting at the Yalta Conference in February 1945 (The Cold War Begins). There was a period of four years between the detonation of the US nuclear weapons in WWII and the detonation of the Soviets first weapon and the beginning of the arms race. Winston Churchill's famous "Iron Curtain" speech was heard on March 5, 1946 and was a defining moment in the division of the Western and Soviet powers. Most people at this time did not realize the Cold War had been in existence for over one year.

The point, is that Cold War II is already being fought and most people do not recognize this fact. The beginning of Cold War II is the day that the US toppled Saddam Hussein in Iraq and stated that major combat operations were complete.

At that time, many Islamic Jihadists entered Iraq to fight the Americans. The Iranian Pasdaran forces also entered the country with the intent of harassing the occupation forces, generating sympathy for the Muslim plight against the "Imperial" Western Forces and attempting to destabilize any attempt at Iraqi self governance. The Pasdaran insurgency was initiated to allow Iran to gain the dominant position in the Gulf Region. It is similar to the Soviet insurgency of Western Europe and the US government in which devout communists were employed by the US government in which they were able to achieve upper level positions.[138]

Insurgency and counter-revolution are common terms that were used frequently during the First Cold War. The quest for Iranian nuclear weapons is similar to the massive intelligence and espionage operations the Soviets launched in their search for nuclear technology. It appears when Iran does develop a nuclear device, an Atomic Curtain will fall over the Middle East. One side will attempt to contain and balance the terror. The other side will attempt to escalate the situation. A form of Détente will be explored with the stakes being raised each time a new weapon is built in Iran.

The balance of power will initially be the deterrent effect that the US and Israel may have on Iran. However, the North Koreans may try to become involved and threaten world peace with their version of nuclear blackmail. China and Russia will be in a position between the US and Iran, as they had both assisted Iran in the development of their nuclear program, but will be unwilling to deflate the situation. The US and Israel will be blamed for the situation as being the aggressors. The European countries that were reluctant to be involved in the war against Iraq in 2003 will, in ideology, be behind the US and Israel, but will be on the sidelines just as they were before. Nevertheless, the Middle East and to a lesser degree, the world will be affected in one form or another. Although Iran is a Muslim country, the government is at odds with other Muslim states and there is a sharp division between the Sunnis and the Shi'as. But with the US and Israel involved, other Islamic governments are bound to be included in the escalating events surrounding the Persian Gulf.

The sphere of influence in the region will be dependent on each country's ability to recognize the dangerous game Iran will play. If Pakistan and Iran relations become closer, India will undoubtedly feel threatened and the flashpoint in Kashmir may ignite. Should Hamas and Hezbollah be identified with Iran, they would undoubtedly feel emboldened and more willing to strike Israel and the US escalating the tension in the Israeli-Palestinian conflict. If Iraq does not remain a strong ally of the US after the American military leaves, they may be caught up in a Shi'a revolution with Iran's backing. Iraq will indeed be the battleground for years to come, both militarily and politically. The effects on each country involved will be severe and the region will be ripe for cataclysmic disaster as Islamic Militants ideology and terror events continue to escalate.

Economic Effects

In economic terms, Iran will continue to suffer international sanctions and embargoes. With the escalation of tension in the region, political and cultural ties with nearby nations will improve. Seeing the US as a common enemy, Militant governed countries will view the political standoff, not as action against a terrorist state, but against a Muslim state with the sovereign right to defend itself with nuclear weapons. A continuing hot war of insurgency will prevail in Iraq even with the replacement of US troops by a UN peacekeeping force.

Just as Roosevelt felt it was necessary to confront the Soviet Union in the UN and not on the battlefield, the European powers will opt to negotiate with Iran in the UN. Meanwhile, to avoid the sting of the sanctions and embargoes, Iran will turn to other means of supplying itself with needed items. In the past, despite the emplacement of sanctions on Iraq, France, Germany and Russia decided to ignore the sanctions and allow business dealings to occur. Avenues of trade with Iraq circumvented the sanctions by using a third party to ship goods. If the governments of these nations remain true to their historical past, they will circumvent the sanctions with Iran as well.

Economically, Iraq, with its ongoing insurgency problem backed by Iran, will be depressed and a victim of nationwide violence designed to destabilize the economy and drive out foreign investors.

Politically, the world community in Cold War II will be divided into three camps. The US, Israel and its allies that strongly oppose Iran and its nuclear proliferation and nuclear blackmail policies will be on one side – the Nuclear Containment side. Iran and radical Muslim countries that oppose the US will be in another – the Nuclear Proliferation side. This will include terrorist organizations such as Hamas, Hezbollah and fringe elements such as the PLO, al Qaeda, and Palestinian Islamic Jihad. A third side, one in which no active participation, with either the US led coalition or the Proliferation Side will be the Appeasers. This group will constantly undermine attempts to contain the Islamic Republic Nuclear Sphere and will continue trade and remain friendly with them. This group of appeasers will include France, Germany, Russia, Canada, China, Japan and other countries in Central Asia, such as Uzbekistan, Khazakstan, Turkmenistan and Tajikistan.

Although the Central Asia nations are predominately Muslim, they do not identify with the foreign policy of Iran. Because of the long period of Soviet domination and oppression in Central Asia, Muslims are "re-learning" Islam. During the time of Soviet oppression, Islam was an underground religion with persecution common place. As the Central Asian nations become more comfortable with their cultural heritage and Islamic roots, they may become more active in international politics. During Cold War II they will probably remain as appeasers so that Iran will not view them as an enemy.

As with the First Cold War, there will be limited overt military maneuvering and/or active operations or direct action except for

"Flashpoints" that will occur as each side pushes the other. This force reconnaissance will manifest itself in small clashes and battles in the ongoing Global War on Terror and the ensuing Cold War II.

Flashpoint: Iraq

The exception will be the ongoing insurgency in Iraq. As long as foreign (US/UN/Non-Muslim) presence remains in the country, a 'hot war' will exist. The Iranian IRGC will maintain a presence in Iraq to continue to the fight against the western occupation forces including the UN. US Special Operations forces will continue to conduct the military portion of the counterrevolution as well as well direct raids and attacks on enemy terrorist cells in Iraq and the surrounding region. The major democratic goal of the Coalition and now the New Iraq Government is a free election in January 2005. The escalation of violence to disrupt the elections and the assassination attempts on prominent figures will increase to the point that the US and UN may agree on a peace-keeping force to provide security. While over the summer of 2004, most attacks were carried out by Ba'athist party members from the former regime, Iranian officers were discovered in Iraq trying to detonate a car bomb. These actions will continue as long as the terror sponsors are allowed to remain in power. Steve Pomerantz (Former FBI head of counter terrorism) and Marc Ginsberg (former Ambassador to Morocco) appeared on Fox News on June 22, 2004 and among other items they discussed, agreed that the single most important country involved in sponsoring terrorism was Iran. …"to defeat worldwide Islamic Terrorism, we must make the government of Iran change its policy in that regard (referring to State Sponsored Terrorism)".

Flashpoint: Syria

The American people are divided on the motivation and result of the war in Iraq. One of the premises of the invasion was that Saddam Hussein had weapons of mass destruction and was in a position to use them. There had been a time period in which the Iraqis were able to hide or move the WMD components. Because the US has been able to find little evidence of the weapons, the logical assumption is that they have been moved. Moved to where? The answer –most likely Syria.

Syria had been a staunch ally of Iraq, and the two governments were politically aligned through the Ba'athist party. An initial article dated May 20, 2004 on Worldnetdaily.com, stated that the WMD were transported to Syria. However, apparently not enough evidence was found to confront the Syrian leader President Bashar Assad on the issue. CIA director George Tenet, National Security Advisor Condoleeza Rice and Secretary of State Colin Powell all agreed that there was not enough evidence to conclude that the weapons had been transferred.[139]

In another article by Worldnetdaily, dated May 20, 2004, new evidence was provided to verify that the weapons had been moved to Syria and then into the Bekaa Valley in Lebanon. The convoys travelling from Iraq to Syria prior to the war were spotted by US satellites and were later verified to be carrying WMD components and platforms by Iraqi scientists and technicians. Apparently, the Syrians agreed to receive the WMD and were paid $30 million to store the weapons. A Syrian defector told US intelligence that the weapons were being held in the Bekaa Valley in huge trenches near Syrian Air Force installations. The Syrians have, per the reports, kept the dual use nuclear technology while transporting the chemical and biological weapons to Lebanon.[140]

The anti-Israeli and anti-US terrorist groups Hezbollah, Islamic Jihad and al Qaeda have trained in terrorist camps located in the Bekaa Valley.[141] Whereas the Syrians have denied their involvement in hiding the WMD, they have hidden the weapons in an area that is populated by members of some of the deadliest terrorist groups in the world. Should it be confirmed or verified that future terrorist attacks with chemical or biological weapons did indeed come from the Bekaa Valley, Syria would be considered a major enemy of the US and would earn its place in the "Axis of Evil". The evidence of chemical and biological weapons in Syria could be a flashpoint for Iran-US conflict as Syria enjoys a close relationship with the Mullahs of the Guardian Counsel.

Flashpoint: Afghanistan

A large amount of saber rattling will be heard on the Iraq-Iran border and if the US increases its presence in Afghanistan to combat insurgents, the common border between Afghanistan and Iran may be a flashpoint. Afghanistan borders Iran on the eastern aspect of the country and a hostile neighbor, or a progressively active border, may induce Iran to take action.

The border area is difficult to secure and a large amount of illegal drugs are smuggled through the border of Iran with a final destination of Europe and the US. This may be done with the consent of the Mullahs in an attempt to destabilize the West in yet another, unconventional method. With a crackdown on drugs and the actions of Afghani warlords, the President of Afghanistan, Hamid Karzai has vowed to stop the illegal drug trade. This action will be headed by US forces with Afghani forces participating and undoubtedly will be located near the Iran border.

This area has a high probability of becoming a flashpoint as the tension between the US and Iran escalates. The Warlords in Afghanistan do not want to give up their territory or weapons and power. The government controls only a portion of the country and the Taliban are trying to make a comeback. All of the factors are important details concerning Iran in dealing with Afghanistan.

Flashpoint: Pakistan

It was the Pakistani intelligence organization that recruited, trained and supported the Taliban. After the attacks of September 11, 2001 and the subsequent war in Afghanistan, the Pakistani government completely changed its view on the Taliban and sided with the US in the GWOT. President Musharef has been supporting the US in its efforts to find Usama bin Laden, but have been very reluctant to allow US forces into Pakistan. While anti-terror operations continue along the Pakistan/ Afghanistan border, the people of Pakistan, predominantly Muslim are showing aggressive signs of dissatisfaction with his leadership. Although most of the extremist schools and social centers have been shut down in Pakistan, the radical Islamic Militant attitude still permeates the populace. The Iranian IRGC is no doubt involved in recruiting extremists for the insurgency that is brewing in places like Karachi, Islamabad, Quetta and Peshawar. Should the extremist elements gain more than a foothold, the stability of an Islamic nuclear country may be at risk. A Pakistani civil war between the extremists and the loyalist would most certainly be a very bloody and prolonged struggle. The area of Kashmir would no doubt destabilize with the military of India moving into the contested area. With intermittent and intense fighting in the highest battlefield of the world, (elevation ranges from 10,000 to 28,250 feet above sea level), the spark that could ignite the region in nuclear catastrophe could begin here.

Flashpoint: Israel

The EU has already made an issue of the terrorism in Iran, the terrorist attacks on Israel and the insidious division it has created in the Middle East. Iran has stated that, when the Islamic Republic has in its possession sometime in the future a nuclear device, it should immediately be used on Israel.

Israel has been the target of debate and attack for decades since its inception in 1948. A major player in the international affairs of the region, Israel is the only democracy in the region and therefore, because of similar beliefs, values and goals, the US has been an ally for years. The Arab and Islamic countries in the region have attempted on numerous occasions to destroy Israel in limited conventional wars such as the 1948 war of independence, the 1956 Sinai Campaign, the 1967 Six-day War, the Yom Kippur War. The Israeli offensive in 1982 - Operation Peace for Galilee - was launched to remove the PLO from southern Lebanon.[142]

The subsequent result of the multiple invasions included the military conquest of areas involved in the fighting which include the areas of Judea, Samaria, the Sinai Peninsula, the Golan heights, and the Gaza strip. Israel kept the gains it had made during these defensive wars. In a controversial decision these gains were approved by the UN. The UN Security Council Resolution 242 provided "acknowledgement of the sovereignty, territorial integrity and political independence of every state in the area and their right to live in peace with secure and recognized boundaries free from threats or acts of force".[143] However, the flashpoint in Israel is not necessarily the lands captured during military episodes, but rather the existence of Israel itself. Less than 24 hours after the State of Israel was proclaimed according to the UN partition plan, the military forces of five Arab countries attacked with the intention of destroying Israel.

The actions of Hezbollah, Hamas, Palestinian Islamic Jihad, Iran, Syria and like minded governments such as Saudi Arabia are still, in a variety of ways, trying to destroy Israel. As long as Israel exists, the Islamic Militants and their supporters will use force in and around Israel to destroy it.

Flashpoint: Central Asia

Islamic countries in Central Asia did not receive the Islamic Revolution from Iran with open arms even as the President of Iran brought the ideology with him. The former Soviet republics in Central Asia have been Muslim for many years before the Bolsheviks proclaimed their communist ideology the grand master of these countries. During the Soviet occupation, the Islamic religion was forced underground with little contact with the outside world.

After the fall of the USSR, the Islamic republics such as Uzbekistan, Khazakstan, Turkmenistan, and Tajikistan were visited by the Iranians in their attempt to export the Islamic Revolution. Tajikistan in particular, it was thought, had a common link to Iran through the Persian language. However, the countries of Central Asia did not receive the Iranian message well. The Tajik civil war forced Iran to take the side of the Russians due to their ongoing relationship with the Bushehr nuclear program. Iran did help to end the war, but it was due to its close ties with Russia that a swift end was reached. The Central Asian area is predominantly Sunni, and the Mullahs realized that the Shi'a doctrine would not be popular. Iran's main enemies in the Central Asian area are the Sunni extremists in Pakistan, the Islamic Movement of Uzbekistan (IMU) and the Taliban in Afghanistan. These extremists lean toward the Wahabism form of Islam and denounce the Shi'as as kafirs or non-believers.

Tensions between Iran and Uzbekistan can be a spark to engulf the entire region in war. The IMU is the largest and most potent Sunni based Islamic Militant group in Uzbekistan and poses a real threat to that country's government. [144] The on-again-off-again relationship that the Uzbek government has with Iran makes this a potential flashpoint with devastating consequences. On July 31, 2004, attacks on the US and Israeli Embassies in Uzbekistan seem to confirm the idea that the Muslim extremists have identified themselves with anti-government forces to attack the Great Satan and the Lesser Satan. The attacks were speculated to have been the work of the Islamic Militants in protest of a trial of their colleagues by the Uzbekistan government.

Flashpoint: Europe

Islamic militants continuously call for attacks on Europe and the West. The militants openly call for a Jihad and the rule of Islam in Europe. An article by Patrick Tyler and Don Van Natta dated April 26, 2004, reported that hundreds of Islamic men in Europe are being recruited into al Qaeda and its affiliated groups. It appears that the "fervor for militancy is intensifying and becoming more open..."[145] It is generally known that in Europe, the Islamic Militants are using more and more converts to Islam that are European to attack.[146] One infamous example of this activity is the Shoe Bomber attack. Richard Reid is a British born Muslim that converted while in jail. He was wrestled to the floor and pummeled into submission by passengers on the flight that he was trying to destroy with plastic explosive in his shoe. He was later convicted of trying to down a plane with a "shoe bomb".[147]

Rohan Gunaratna states in his book *Inside al Qaeda, Global Network of Terror,* that most al Qaeda operatives in Europe are European Muslims, that 'there are more than enough operatives in Europe to carry out plans such as recruitment, credit card fraud, robbery and assassination'. [148]

The range of the Iranian Shahab 3 missile puts Western Europe in the middle of the sights of the Mullahs of Iran. Should any European country attempt to forcibly stop the Iranians from carrying out their nuclear program, or attempt to persuade Iran to abandon its terrorist sponsorship, or pressure the Mullah government on the Human Rights issues, they could be targeted with ballistic and cruise missiles possibly armed with nuclear weapons.

Flashpoint: USA

A professional dedicated terrorist group has gained access to the US and attacked New York and the Pentagon in a horribly effective suicide attack. Other attacks that al Qaeda can use are conventional explosives or hit and run type tactics. Target systems involved would include those to destabilize the local, state and federal governments. The fact that al Qaeda and others have attacked targets both in the US (9/11 attacks) and overseas

(US Embassies, etc), indicates their attacks are not well coordinated if they truly wish to destabilize the government.

However, economically, the US could be damaged simply due to the lack of commerce after a terrorist attack. It is estimated that the attacks of September 11, 2001 cost the US economy $639 billion and 2 million lost jobs.[149] The economy bounced back fairly quickly due to the resolve of the American people and it would take a truly devastating attack to bring down the economy.

Islamic Militants live and work in the US and circulate their dangerous ideology and are allowed to do so under the 1st Amendment rights. These individuals may increase their ability to destabilize the government system by taking advantage of US freedoms. Such ability can increase with individual state legislation that proposes to give an undocumented immigrant a driver's license. How does this destabilize the government? The one document that is required to purchase a firearm in each state is the driver's license or identification card. How would the State or Federal government be able to track undocumented immigrants with a driver's license? It is unknown at this time, but in effect, the passage of a driver's license bill for undocumented immigrants would be tantamount to giving a potential terrorist a government-issued document to travel the country with legally purchased firearms. The flashpoint in the US will centered on the militants' rhetoric and hit and run tactics. It has been speculated that the US will not fall from outside invaders, but from legislation which limits the ability to protect itself internally. The above information seems to corroborate that speculation.

Flashpoint: Iran

The danger of Iran being involved in a conflict with the US has a high potential when the issue of the nuclear program is concerned. The US and Israel have already stated on numerous occasions that a nuclear armed Iran is not an option. The Israelis have attacked Iraq's nuclear program and destroyed the Osirak nuclear reactor near Baghdad in 1981 which put a halt to nuclear research in Iraq. The US is undoubtedly considering a similar approach based on the success of the Israelis. The Iranians are very adamant about the international implications of an attack on their nuclear facilities and have stated that they would retaliate against the attackers. Israel will defend itself if Iran attacks with missiles which could involve other 'special' package deployments of chemical or biological weapons. The US has deployed anti-missile assets in Israel for this contingency. However, the US would probably suffer retaliation in the form of a series of terrorist attacks. The escalation of violence due to the Iranian nuclear program may become a major flashpoint for nuclear war should the US or Israel attack the Iranians. The Iranians may use any nuclear weapons in retaliation. Therefore it is imperative to act sooner rather than later.

Chapter Eleven
Cold War I Vs Cold War II

The First Cold War was known for its covert intelligence operations that and its harrowing stories of bravery and escape. Cold War II will involve incessant intelligence gathering missions as well. Human assets on the ground will be the most important aspect of the intelligence initiative. While in the First Cold War, technology and spy satellites were a dominant feature of intelligence gathering, the human factor in the Middle East will be much more important because of the lack of hardware and technology in the region.

Most of Iran's target systems have already been identified and will be monitored closely. Monitoring, identifying and verifying nuclear components, technology and weapons will be increased with the escalating events. Assets on the ground can provide quick response and definitive answers whereas the technological intelligence gathered from equipment such as spy satellites, digital imaging and spy planes, both manned and unmanned must be analyzed at several levels.

Conversely, defections of key personnel in the First Cold War were abundant. In the Second Cold War, defections will probably not be as numerous. Mostly this is because of the religious background of the government of Iran and the nuclear experts that are employed. It seems that, because the Iranian government has had to build its nuclear program from scratch, they would be reluctant to use individuals that were not absolutely loyal to the Islamic Revolution. Russia has been training technicians for the reactor facility in Bushehr in Russia out of the sphere of influence of the Iranian government. No defections or activities out of the ordinary have been reported. There appear to be no influences or enticement for the scientists or technicians to leave their country for political or monetary reasons.

Communications security during the current Cold War has advanced far beyond anything anyone during the first Cold War could have imagined. The secret codes that constantly change to prevent the enemy from deciphering messages are still around and very much needed. However, the messages are encoded by computer encoding programs and sent with burst technology over satellite communications equipment to be decoded by advanced technology. However, the Iranian communications network is not as advanced and could be a weak link in its defense. The advantage here lies with the US.

A need for missile technology exists for new nuclear nations. Both Iran and North Korea are actively developing and testing new missile designs to mount nuclear, chemical and biological payloads. North Korea has tested the Taepodong 1 missile in 1998 and is in the process of developing the Taepodong 2 missile which has a range of 5000 miles.[150] Iran has been trading with North Korea for years and it should be understood that Tehran is actively trying to acquire missile technology. Iran is in the process of developing its own missiles called the Shahab-4 which is based on Russian SS-4 missile technology and has a range of about 3600 kms.[151]

In the first Cold War, the Soviets and Chinese were initially active in trading missile and weapons technology so that similar military products have been produced in both countries. After WWII, the Soviets managed to forcibly convince ex-Nazi rocket specialists to work for the Warsaw Pact.

It was through the acquisition of German technology that the Soviets were able to develop workable missiles to mount nuclear warheads. Werner von Braun was the prominent German rocket scientist that worked with the US missile program and later the Apollo space program. Using knowledge and experience from the pool of German WWII scientists, the new super powers were able to compete in the Cold War arms race. The Iranians are using technicians from other countries just as their Cold War predecessors did.

The saber rattling from Iran is becoming more prominent and resembles the claims made between the USSR and the US on the space race. Now it appears Iran will attempt to launch a satellite into space within the next 18 months. Iran's defense minister, Ali Shamkani, stated on January 6th, 2004, that "…Iran will be the first Islamic country to enter the stratosphere with its own satellite, and its own indigenous launch system".[152] He may be speaking of a three-stage rocket that can launch a 'payload' into space. This 'space technology' attempt may be a clever way of disguising its attempt to create an inter-continental ballistic missile.

The saber rattling and positioning has begun in earnest and is not difficult to see. Evidence of Cold War II is most recently reflected in the statements made by Iran's president Khatami: "Possessing technology for the nuclear fuel cycle is our right and nobody can deny us of this right under international regulations", He also stated, "We will continue cooperation with the IAEA as long as our interests require and as long as we know various plots led by the US are ineffective".[153]

The Al Jazeera Global News reports on March 17, 2004, that the US is politically divided in its decision on beginning talks with Iran and normalizing relations. In the same article, the diplomatic offer which has become known as "Iran's Grand Bargain" would discuss concerns over nuclear arms, terrorism and the Israeli- Palestinian conflict. In return the US is expected to lift sanctions, not refer to Iran as part of the Axis of Evil and not pursue a "regime change" in an effort to re-establish relations. [154] Interestingly, these are the three items that must be pursued to stop Iran from producing nuclear weapons.

However, when the devastating earthquake hit the eastern Iranian City of Bam, the Iranian government initially refused assistance from US civilian and humanitarian organizations. With the devastation so great, some US civilian rescue teams were allowed in to help along with humanitarian aid. Ayat Allah Ahmad Jannati is the head of Iran's Guardian Council and stated on January 3, 2004, "Naturally America wanted to take advantage of this situation [the earthquake disaster in Bam] by offering some help and bringing up the issue of relations". He continued, "But it was given a slap in the face...Death to America". President Khatami has stated that the sending of American aid was "not a harbinger of better ties" with Iran and he went on to say that US officials "talk a lot of nonsense". [155] If the Iran is not willing to engage the US on humanitarian grounds, why would they engage the US with its "Grand bargain"?

Hot War versus Cold War

When one thinks of the First Cold War, the hot spots of that time are the police action in Korea, the foreign internal defense action in the Republic of Vietnam and the invasion of Afghanistan by the Soviets in 1979. These 'hot wars' have involved dozens of countries and devastated the surrounding regions.

The Korean War was fought by countries as part of a coalition of forces under the UN flag against North Korea and China. The political history of the Korea peninsula after WWII was a direct result of the Yalta Conference in 1945, which, incidentally, is the recognized start of the First Cold War. After the Japanese were defeated in 1945, Korea was divided along the 38th parallel into North and South with the USSR administratively in charge of the North and the United States administratively running South Korea. Because of the ideological divide in the political systems, the US was an advocate of a democratic government in South Korea and the USSR was strong proponent of a socialistic model of government similar to its own in North Korea. During this time the Soviets and Chinese had differing view points on the implementation of communism and socialism which resulted in political confrontation between the two.

In 1950, North Korea invaded the South with the intent of unifying Korea under one socialist government. With the mobilization of UN forces including the US, the communists were pushed back past the 38th parallel and into North Korea. The US Marines had pushed all the way through North Korea to the Yalu River on the Red Chinese border with the intent of establishing a base of operations near the Chosen Reservoir. At that point the communist Chinese launched an attack of 300,000 'volunteers' into North Korea against the UN forces which were driven back to about the 38th parallel. Several major battles ensued over territory along the 38th parallel until a cease fire agreement was signed in 1953. This hot war of political ideology; communist style socialism versus the UN member's politically mixed democratically elected governments and old world monarchies, was one of the most intense political struggles in the latter half of the Twentieth Century. The fighting involving dozens of countries from all corners of the world in an effort to contain the communist aggression.

The Strategy of the Communists during the First Cold War was to infiltrate a country, start an insurgency, convince the people that they were being taken advantage of by the ruling elite or the foreign influences and overthrow the government. The Communist sympathizers would then hijack the interim government and rule the country with a Socialist style government.

In Vietnam, after WWII, the French were fighting the Viet Minh which were determined to send the French back to Europe after 70 years of colonialism. This area was ripe for revolution as the Vietnamese were looking for an independent state government. Ho Chi Minh, backed by the

Soviet Union after WWII, fought the French and finally defeated Foreign Legion troopers at Dien Bien Phu. In the 1960's, President Kennedy, eager to contain the expansion of Communism, sent troops to assist the South Vietnamese with their internal defense. The unconventional style of warfare with which the Viet Cong and the communists fought in that war was a much different type of fighting than what the western powers had been prepared for. Again, this was a war of containment involving ideology of communism versus the free world, led by the United States.

In Afghanistan, the government was overthrown in 1978 and a socialist state emerged. It was strong on ideology, but weak in political and military power. They asked for help from the Soviet Union, which according to some, invaded the country in 1979 somewhat reluctantly. Also not prepared for the fierce resistance and the unconventional style of warfare, the Soviets were fighting a war of communist ideology versus guerillas that based their fight on religious grounds. The Muslim Ummah of Afghanistan were under attack by the Soviets and the religion prescribed that able-bodied Muslims join the fight to destroy the enemy. In secret political and covert military operations, the US assisted the Muslim mujahideen in their long fight for freedom.

In each case, the ideology of the oppressive communists versus the governments of the world that had free will was the basis of these wars. Today, in Cold War II, the same is true. The authoritarian theocratic government of Iran and its sphere of influence is at odds with the UN and the US.

The danger to the world and the main topic at issue is the production of dual use nuclear technology. In a November 14, 2003 article in *National Review Online*, Amir Taheri stated in Recipe for Disaster "Iran's national defense doctrine has been based on the assumption that it will one day fight a war with United Stated, plus its Arab allies and Israel".[156]

In comparison, of the two Cold Wars, Cold War II is well under way and two wars have been fought. Now the ongoing insurgency in Iraq and the attempted resurgence of the Taliban in Afghanistan have developed into two flashpoints that are flanking Iran. This violence is spreading and now involves Central Asia as demonstrated in the bombings of the Israeli and US embassies.

These Cold War II hotspots are yielding information about the enemy and their backers. For instance; the type of offensive capability Iran possesses and how it views itself in the Gulf region are important elements. Pasdaran forces are actively working in Iraq and nearby countries in the region, including Afghanistan, and are escalating the tension in the area. Additionally, Iran's military commander believes that a military confrontation with the US is the only serious threat to Iran's sovereignty. Iran has also commented on several scenarios in the region in which Israel will be targeted.

"In a nuclear duel in the region, Israel may kill 100 million Muslim. Muslims can sustain such casualties, knowing that in exchange, there would be no Israel on the map", stated Former Iranian President Hashemi Rafsanjani in October 2000.[157] If a conflict were to take place, according to Taheri, the Iranians believe that the US cannot sustain a long involved war. After trying to use hit and run, guerilla style unconventional tactics to increase the American casualties, the Iranians would brandish its nuclear weapons and use the threat of nuclear war as a means of forcing the US into a truce and removing its troops from the region. [158]

Paper Tiger

The Iranians and Usama bin Laden believe that the US is a paper tiger and cannot stomach a long protracted war. They believe the US cannot sustain operations for more than a couple of years. Using the strategy above, in their view, would humiliate the US and drive them out of the Persian Gulf.

The Iranians appear to base this strategy on three events of the past that involved the Peacekeeping forces in Lebanon in 1983, the first Persian Gulf War and the UN operations in Somalia. The most recent war in Iraq, they feel, was an easy victory and does not show the world the true nature of the US.

First, the US Marines and French Foreign Legion forces in the peacekeeping force present in Beirut, Lebanon in 1983, were attacked by vehicle bombs and suffered hundreds of casualties. The vivid videotape and photographs of Americans injured and dead in the rubble of their barracks was too much for the US public to bear. This idea was amplified by the mainstream media who were opposed to the Reagan doctrine. Several months later the US withdrew its forces stating the mission was complete. The Muslim world saw this as retreat. After the withdrawal, the Islamic Militants, fresh from their war with the Soviets, viewed the US as a paper tiger and realized that the American public could not stomach a war in which there were a large number of American casualties.

Second, the US led coalition had gone into the First Persian Gulf War with the American public not really believing that a shooting war was about to ensue. There were public demonstrations and an outcry from some fringe elements, but by and large, the public thought that the US would find a way to allow Saddam Hussein to withdrawal his forces. The US had been involved in only minor skirmishes such as Panama, Lebanon, and Grenada since the Vietnam War and the American public was used to a peacetime military in which men and women joined the military to get money for college, not go to war.

Once the shooting war started, the public and politicians opposed to the war started to make their voice heard. The President of the United States also agreed that the war should be limited to liberating Kuwait and the military should come home quickly. President George H. Bush decided that the US would not be involved in another quagmire like the war in

Vietnam was generally viewed. He decided the US could not be involved in a war in which the US would suffer a large number of casualties or be involved in a prolonged struggle in the Mid-East.

The third event involved Task Force Ranger in Somalia in 1993. The combination Ranger/Special Forces detachment was involved in fierce fighting in the Somali capital of Mogadishu while capturing enemy targets. Through the course of an 18-hour battle through the night of October 3-4, 1993 eighteen American soldiers were killed and dozens wounded. Enemy casualties were estimated at 500 killed and over 1000 wounded.[159] Throughout the next day, the bodies of dead American soldiers were stripped and tied and subsequently dragged through the streets of Mogadishu. Scenes of American dead being dragged through the streets of the Somali capital were more than President Clinton could bear. US forces were subsequently withdrawn from the area. The Iranians noted that each time the US suffered casualties, the US President withdrew the forces and attempted to minimize the political controversy.

Iran's strategy, presuming the Americans will withdrawal from the region after taking too many casualties, is to escalate the tension between the two countries. Once the Americans are driven out of Iran and the Persian Gulf, Iran would have absolute control over the Persian Gulf and threaten the existence of Israel and could eventually threaten Europe. Iran currently appears to be the missile superpower of the Middle East and could target any of the countries in the region. "We have enough missiles for a rain of death the likes of which no one has imagined in this part of the world," stated Defense Minister Rear-Admiral Ali Shamkhani.[160]

Persian Gulf Missile Crisis

The Cuban Missile Crisis in 1961 between the super powers involved the positioning of nuclear weapons in Cuba that would be directed at the US should the Soviets wish to launch an attack. For 13 days, the tensions between the US and USSR grew to the point that any further escalation would undoubtedly mean the destruction of the world in a nuclear exchange. The point of contention was the positioning of missiles in an area that would threaten the US and reduce its reaction time to retaliate.

Should Iran decide to push for the domination of the Persian Gulf, missiles - both anti-ship and special application (nuclear or chemical) - placed at the mouth of the Straits of Hormuz could be a flashpoint for nuclear war as well. In this scenario, the anti-ship missiles could easily destroy oil tankers and supply ships moving into the Gulf. If the US follows its previous action, US Navy ships would enter the area to project power from the sea. The Iranians, not wanting to lose face with the international community, would try to engage the US warships with cruise missiles such as the Chinese silkworm missile. Even though US ships have anti-missile defensive capability, They could be damaged or sunk. During the Iran-Iraq war, two French-made Exocet missiles fired from a French built Mirage Iraqi warplane hit and almost sank the USS Stark on March 17, 1987 killing 37 US Navy sailors and officers.

Once fired upon, the US warships would be forced to defend themselves and attack the Iranian missile sites. With improved technology, the Iranians may inflict sufficient damage on the Navy ships so that US military ground forces would attempt to seize the area at the mouth of the Straits of Hormuz. The Iranians, not having a strong enough maritime force to compete with the US, may turn to their nuclear weapons and use them to threaten the US or her allies in the region. Undoubtedly, in the US Navy Task Force, nuclear missile frigates or nuclear missile carrying submarines would be present and in position to threaten Iranian sovereignty. The tension in the area would escalate and an Iranian Missile Crisis could develop.

However, the US and Iran do not have a direct communication system and must go through third parties to communicate. The other option is to verbally spar on the floor of the UN, but this will accomplish little. This missile crisis, due to the lack of communication avenues, may prove to be much more dangerous and volatile than any other nuclear standoff in the past.

Islamic Revolutionary Aggressive Nuclear Sphere (IRANS)

The Warsaw Pact was organized by the Soviet Union to counter the US-European Alliance, which created the North Atlantic Treaty Organization (NATO). The Warsaw Pact countries were led by the USSR and consisted of its 15 republics and the satellite countries of Eastern Europe. Although each country had its indigenous military to protect its borders and territorial interests, the Soviet Union wielded political and strategic power over those countries.

The Islamic Revolutionary Aggressive Nuclear Sphere (IRANS) that would be initiated to control the Persian Gulf and Central Asia would center on Iran. Once Iran has nuclear weapons it will look to other Muslim countries for like minded individuals and governments. Although Pakistan is currently an ally of the US in the GWOT, President Musharef is not popular with the entire population of his country. There are many in his country that would like to see someone who believes in traditional application of Islam law - *sharia*. Should Musharef loose control of the government and an Islamic Militant Revolutionary force come to power, they would no doubt be allied with Iran. Most likely, if there were a popular uprising against Musharef, it would be initiated and spurred on by the Iranian Pasdaran in their effort to export the Islamic Revolution.

A pro-Iranian government in Pakistan would be exactly what Tehran would like to see. With two nuclear armed Islamic countries with militant style governments, one can surmise that a shifting of strategic assets would occur resulting in a larger sphere of influence through Central Asia. The flashpoint in this area would be not only in Kashmir with fighting escalating between Pakistan and India, but also in Uzbekistan. Uzbekistan was sympathetic to the US during the Afghanistan invasion. Iran has surely taken note of this and although intelligence in the area does not

121

reveal a large presence of Pasdaran or Iranian influence in Central Asia, the cultural and religious ties may bring them together or if not, result in confrontation.

Uzbekistan is one of the countries in the region that has an organized and disciplined military and has ties with Washington. Strategically, Iran would need to befriend Uzbekistan or establish some form of control over the government. Currently this is unlikely, but events could change in the future. The Islamic Revolution Aggressive Nuclear Sphere could range from Kazakhstan which borders China to the borders of Turkey and the Black Sea. A bloody civil war and political coup by Tajik Islamic militants in the early 1990's gives reason to western analysts to be concerned with Central Asia. [161]The Iranians were directly involved in that civil war, but to remain on good terms with Russia, helped to end the conflict. Not all Central Asian countries get along and Uzbekistan and Tajikistan have a long history of confrontations. The rise of Islamic Militants is a concern in the strategic sense.

Under the umbrella of the Islamic Revolutionary Aggressive Nuclear Sphere would be the terrorist organizations and Shi'a associates from other countries in the area. Hezbollah, Hamas, Palestinian Islamic Jihad, Ansar al Islam and al Qaeda are just some of the terrorist organizations that would be very useful to the Iranians in the Sphere.

Appeasement breeds escalation

When Premier Khrushchev saw weakness, he pursued and tried to dominate in all he did. This was true in his foreign policy when dealing with President Kennedy during the Cuban Missile Crisis and also in his political views throughout his career. While a political field officer in Stalingrad in 1943, during WWII or the Great Patriotic War as the Soviets called it, Khrushchev dominated the political and ideological arm of the military in that region. It is reported that if he found weakness in his subordinates, he eliminated them and found others to project a strong image.

Later, pushing the envelope of diplomacy during the Cuban Missile Crisis, Khrushchev ignored the US blockade of Cuba and proceeded to establish a nuclear missile base on that island. He only backed down after being confronted with a guarantee of simultaneous nuclear destruction if he continued his 'reckless' course of action. Appeasement leads to escalation. This was true in the First Cold War and is true as well in the Second Cold War.

Another example of "appeasement breeds escalation" occurred in 1973. In the Yom Kippur War in the Arab-Israeli conflict, Syria and Egypt launched an attack that took Israel by surprise. The US was able to assist the Israeli nation with supplies and aid. The Soviet Union was supplying the Arab countries and threatened to send in a large number of troops for "peacekeeping" operations and establish a foothold in the region. Negotiations were going nowhere and it was only when President Nixon raised the Defense Condition of the United States to DefCon 3 (the highest alert in peacetime), did the Soviets back down.[162]

Still another example involves the terrorists. In the Middle East conflict, a summit between Yassar Arafat of the PLO and Israeli Prime Minister Barak in the US at Camp David occurred in July 2000. Barak offered a peace agreement and a Palestinian state to Arafat in return for peace. Barak even offered to divide Jerusalem, which was a goal of Arafat's for some time. However, Arafat walked away from the negotiations and resumed the attacks on Israel with even more violence than has been previously seen.[163] Signs of weakness or appeasement will motivate the Islamic militants to escalate the violence with the goal of destroying their enemy, not co-existing.

Recent terrorist activities including the Madrid train bombings in March 2004, have had a major impact on the national elections in Spain. The Socialist party won and immediately vowed to remove its troops from Iraq. One of the stipulations for declaring victory in the occupied

Arab lands as defined by Usama bin Laden is that Western powers must leave the Land of Mohammed.[164] When Spain removed its troops from Iraq, the Islamic Militants, including the Iranian Revolutionary militant government have sensed weakness in the coalition and are escalating attacks, especially on foreigners. Should the Spanish government decide to try to negotiate or appease the terrorists, the Islamic militants will only increase the frequency of their attacks on high visibility areas such as transportation hubs.

There were a great many Islamic mujahideen that fought in Afghanistan against the Soviet Union in their effort to protect the Muslim Ummah. These mujahideen, no doubt, have learned this attitude of taking advantage of appeasers and the tactic of exploiting the enemy especially when a sign of weakness presents itself.

Chapter Twelve
Fighting the New Cold War

The detailed strategy of fighting the First Cold War varied from President to President. However, the general strategy was that of containment and coexistence. The buzzwords in political circles in Washington DC in the 1970's were 'détente' and 'nuclear freeze'. Détente was a concept that involved the US recognizing the USSR as a nuclear equal and in effect gave the USSR a more active voice in international politics, especially in the case of East and West Germany.

During the period of Détente, 1969-1975, the West German Chancellor Willy Brandt, a Social Democrat visited East Germany and made it clear that the borders of the Iron Curtain were officially recognized. Also a condition of Détente was the Soviet condition that the US have an understanding of the Sino-Russo relations and basically take the Soviet's side. Summits were attended and treaties such as the SALT treaty were proposed. Human rights issues were discussed at the Helsinki meetings and both sides felt they had walked away from the bargaining table with what they needed.[165]

To attain a strong nuclear posture in the world at that time, it took quite a lot of money and an almost inexhaustible source of appropriate resources. Both the US and USSR had been escalating the nuclear arms race by increasing the number of warheads. It was a policy that was draining to both sides. President Reagan changed the policy of nuclear freeze and détente to nuclear arms offensive and Strategic Defense Initiative (SDI).

The promotion of increased nuclear weapons and the fact that SDI would render the Soviet Union's nuclear arsenal impotent was a key factor in the defeat of communism in the Cold War.[166] SDI involved the idea of space borne platforms that would be able to detect and destroy enemy nuclear missiles launched at the US before reaching the US. While the US would be able to effectively defend itself, the Soviets would be sitting ducks for any retaliation by the US. The Soviets were drawn to the negotiating table with the threat of SDI looming over them. Gorbachev and Reagan met several times and a reduction in missiles was proposed by the Soviets. However, Reagan simply walked away from the table putting the Soviet government into a panic. In 1986, the Communist Party announced at the 27th Party Congress that, "without an acceleration of the country's economic and social development, it will be impossible to maintain our position in the international scene".[167]

Reagan took the hard-line and refused to negotiate. His understanding of Soviet determination of world domination was clear and he was able to stand up to and defeat the Soviet aggressors. In 1989, the Berlin Wall fell and the Soviet grip on Eastern Europe was released. Several years later, the Soviet Union fell apart and the nuclear threat that was so prevalent was reduced so dramatically, that the Russians and Americans, in the 'New World Order' were becoming "friends".

Iran is currently under sanctions and embargoes by the US and some UN constituents. However, there are many that trade directly and indirectly with Iran, which allows them to skirt the international political pressure. Russia, China and North Korea are openly trading with Iran and providing not only general items of trade, but also nuclear technology, training and technicians. Canada, a US ally for years has increased its trade with Iran;

in 2003 it totaled over $300 million and is increasing each year.[168] Canada keeps open ties with Iran through its embassy in Tehran. The containment and coexistence policy of the appeasers of the past has allowed Iran to continue to survive and function while exporting its Islamic Revolution. It appears that geopolitical attempts to isolate Iran to bring down its economy and its government have been only partially successful. As events warrant, the US will be forced to change strategy, as the Iranian domination in the Persian Gulf becomes more evident. This change in strategy will be compared retrospectively to the Reagan Doctrine against the Soviets.

Initially, the *change in strategy will be ridiculed by the left and individuals that do not believe Iran is a threat to the Persian Gulf and the US.* While Iran will not compete directly with the US in a nuclear arms race, it will compete with the US in ideology based on the free trade practices of the Persian Gulf countries. It will also brandish its nuclear weapons and missiles in an attempt to explain to the world that Iran is on equal terms with the US as far as nuclear capability in the Persian Gulf. Having the ability and the motivation to launch nuclear weapons at US interests and allies with, what Iran hopes the world perceives, the slightest provocation will completely destabilize the area putting most of the World on the defensive when it comes to the Persian Gulf.

A nuclear standoff policy of containment and détente would ensue and relations would stagnate. A strategic defense for the Persian Gulf will have to be implemented – SDI on a local level with anti-missile assets positioned in the Gulf region by the US to render the Iranian threat impotent. Iranian defenses will have to be destroyed either by covert forces or limited strikes directly against Iran. While the latter is much more dangerous, the idea of rendering the Iranian nuclear arsenal impotent will have a dramatic effect on the politics in the Persian Gulf and the level of oil exported in the region.

Winning the Cold War and the GWOT

The key to reducing the intensity and length of Cold War II lies in prevention of nuclear proliferation, preemptive strikes on countries pursuing proliferation, interdiction of nuclear hardware and technology and cooperation of international coalitions united to stop nuclear proliferation. The key to winning the GWOT is the removal of the terrorists' support and training areas. By stopping nuclear proliferation, the support base of the terrorists can be destroyed too.

The Iranian government believes that war is inevitable with the US and has disclosed their wartime intentions on numerous occasions. Because they believe the US cannot sustain an extended war with high numbers of casualties, Iran believes it can win a war of attrition with the US. However, in review of wars in which the US has participated, the war of attrition has been used by the US against its enemies. The First and Second World Wars, Korea, Vietnam and the First Persian Gulf War were all wars of attrition in which the US had the upper hand of supplies, men and materiel.

There are three points to the Iranian strategy of Persian Gulf domination that are imperative.

-Iran has a large army with over 20 million troops that can be mobilized from the population. They feel that the US is outnumbered and their strategy used in the Iran/Iraq war of 1980-88 will induce enough fear in the US to not attack.

- Iran has the most missiles in the Persian Gulf region and will, at the direction of the Mullahs, use them to destroy strategic assets in the Gulf. This strategy is based on their previous use of missiles in the Iran/Iraq war.

-Iran feels that the nuclear weapon capability is a deterrent and that it can use the weapons in place of its conventional military. It is estimated that they can produce a nuclear weapon within 18 months.[169]

The strategy that Iran will most likely favor brings millions of men and thousands of missiles to the battlefield. However, the human wave charges of men and boys into the Iraqi defenses were tactically disastrous and were of very little use strategically. Therefore, despite Iran's bold but stupid waste of human life, the nuclear question must be dealt with quickly and severely. The alternative is the domination of the Persian Gulf by Iran and the proliferation of nuclear technology and weapons throughout Central Asia.

Prevention

Prevention of nuclear proliferation is a responsibility of the world community and involves the International Atomic Energy Agency as the chief institution responsible for inspecting and verifying nuclear related hardware, technology and fuel disposal. A consistent program to monitor Iran needs to be in place. Blocking the inspectors is one stall tactic used by Iraq in deception programs and Iran seems to have started to employ this tactic as well.

In March 2004, Iran blocked IAEA inspectors from entering the country after the UN issued a censure against Iran because of their deception involving the nuclear program. Reluctance of Russia, China, North Korea and other countries to heed the political advice of the US not to assist in the proliferation of nuclear technology is a major roadblock to the unified goal of stopping nuclear proliferation. Negotiations with Russia and China must continue on the subject of preventing nuclear proliferation. At the very least, North Korea must be contained and the technology it exports must be prevented from reaching other non-nuclear countries.

Preemption and Interdiction

Preemption and interdiction are two methods of dealing with countries that don't adhere to the UN's International treaty on nuclear non-proliferation. Preemptive operations against the production of nuclear weapons or plans to produce nuclear weapons are an option for not just the US, but any country that does not wish to see the proliferation of nuclear weapons. Israel attacked the Iraqi Tammuz1 (Osirak) nuclear reactor near Baghdad on June 7, 1981 to stop Saddam Hussein from continuing his quest for nuclear technology and weapons.[170] If the tension in the Persian Gulf escalates due to the proliferation of nuclear power, more strikes such as these will occur.

Interdiction of the supply route to Iran must be interrupted. The supplies that reach Iran are through other country avenues and need to be closed. As in the late 1980s, US and Coalition ships can interdict supply ships to Iranian harbors. Interdiction of the waterways can be accomplished by the US Navy and Coast Guard detachments in the Persian Gulf and should be stepped up immediately. Supply ships entering the waters near Iranian harbors must be searched and illegal shipments seized. A coordinated attack plan should be in place before Iran can obtain the fuel that will run the reactors. Other than maritime operations, border operations and special operations to stop the overland route of nuclear hardware and technology can be used, but may cross the line at international relations with Iran's bordering neighbors.

Interdiction of key personnel is another option to stop the nuclear process from continuing. Although extremely controversial, the elimination of the key nuclear personnel and/or technicians would have a direct effect on the nuclear program. Although, the kidnapping or killing of nuclear personnel breaches international law, the option still exists. The US initiated the Phoenix program in Vietnam to eliminate key Viet Cong and North Vietnamese personnel including cell leaders, weapons and communication personnel and tax collectors. The operation had many successes and was effective in meeting its goals of denying the enemy the use of their trained personnel. As stated this is highly controversial and illegal, however, if the US and the EU believe that Iran is producing a nuclear weapon for the specific use of killing Americans and Europeans (versus a political deterrent affect), then there may be no choice. Covert action such as this is very effective.

International Cooperation

The key to all of the preventative measures is cooperation of allies and governments in the region with the US. Cooperation translates to support, as the US is a leader in the Global War on Terror, and it is doubtful that any other country would take the leadership position of the US. The EU and others must recognize the danger that Iran poses to the world as the US has pointed out on numerous occasions. The US does not have the manpower, currently, to monitor the borders of Iran or to provide in depth surveillance on, or to board each ship in the Persian Gulf. Allies such as the UK, Australia and others can aid the US in stopping the proliferation of the weapons technology in this area, but more cooperation from friendly countries that share our vision are needed. There is a reluctance of European nations to follow the lead of the US in matters pertaining to the Persian Gulf and it appears the US and the UK will be forced to confront Iran on this issue. In short, the EU must cooperate with the US. The EU and the US must work from a common platform when it comes to Iranian nuclear proliferation.

Countries that are aligned in the Appeaser category of Cold War II will be the ones complaining the loudest and the most often in the UN. But if the Cold War of the past is any indication of how the countries in the world will align, the US and the UK have the most weight on their shoulders. Liberals and anti-Iraq war protesters may have a vision of peace in the world, but to believe that the Islamic militants would not use nuclear weapon on the US is naive. The rhetoric of the Iranians and violent ties they have with the terrorists indicates that they would use any means necessary to destroy their enemies (Israel and the US).

So the key to preventing Iran from obtaining or using nuclear weapons once they are obtained is cooperation between the EU, Russia, Central Asia, China and of course the middle Eastern countries including Saudi Arabia and the newly formed Iraq, with the US in the lead. Such a challenge is daunting, but not unobtainable. It is important to get these nations to recognize there is a major political and potentially life-threatening problem in the Persian Gulf and it is called Iran. The US should continue to be a leader, as it is currently, in confronting the despotic regime of Iran and stopping the nuclear proliferation. As stated earlier, a common platform must be agreed upon and then a set of achievable goals to stop Iran or control the nuclear program it wants to create.

Containment and Rollback

Containment would involve strategy of the First cold war in which the US and its allies contained the expansion of communism and the proliferation of nuclear weapons that the Soviets were initiating. The Carter Doctrine was aimed at containing Iran and its ideology. Despite his best efforts, President Carter's containment policy did not contain Iran, but did stop the USSR from moving into the Persian Gulf. The US has, in the past, confronted and contained nuclear powers such as the USSR and North Korea, so the containment of ideology is not the issue. The Iranian Islamic Revolution ideology was contained by the Islamic beliefs of the Sunnis and Wahabis. The dominance of the Sunni sect of the religion precluded the Shi'a ideology and the Khomeini revolutionary process from succeeding in other countries. The issue is whether the US can stop Iran from using the weapons once it has them.

Rollback Iran has begun its attempt to produce an indigenous fuel cycle so that it will be dependent on outside assistance to maintain its nuclear energy program and to continue its attempt at establishing the infrastructure for nuclear weapons production. Prevention is designed to stop the pursuit of nuclear weapons. Containment is designed to control the nuclear dilemma and aggressive ideology in the Persian Gulf. Rollback is a concept that is designed to convince the Mullahs that having and maintaining a nuclear program is either too expensive, or not in the best interest of Iran. If successful, Iran would either give up or scale back its attempts at producing nuclear weapons. Developing a nuclear program with an indigenous nuclear fuel cycle is very expensive and involves a great deal of planning, protection and coordination. One of the provisions of the Non-proliferation Treaty is the intention of nuclear capable countries to provide technological assistance to a non-nuclear capable country with the restriction that it will not produce its own weapons. Because of these stipulations it is concerning that the Islamic theocracy has decided to embark on its own attempt to produce a fuel cycle. In theory, once the fuel cycle is complete, the enrichment process of the uranium is the final hurtle in producing nuclear weapons. But as stated, the NPT prohibits signatory nations from resigning from the treaty to produce nuclear weapons unless an imminent threat is present.

However, North Korea was able to obtain all the materials, fuel and technology without violating any rules of the NPT. When it was ready, it suddenly withdrew from the NPT and began producing nuclear weapons and has been producing between 2 and 5 weapons per year for the past several years.[171]

Convincing Iran that it should not produce nuclear weapons and to 'rollback' its production and nuclear power capability is a great challenge. The government of Iran has been convinced that it has needed nuclear power for some time and began its quest for the program shortly after the 1979 revolution.

Russia and, to a lesser degree, China have been supplying Iran with everything they will need to develop nuclear power and eventually nuclear weapons. Russia has been insistent that it can control the fuel source and disposal process of the enriched uranium fuel that it is providing to Iran.

This situation has led many governments to believe that they will have to live with a nuclear capable Iran. The nuclear industry is a very lucrative one for Russia and with the right customer, Russia realized it could cash in on its Cold War technology. Iran has the desire and finances to be the perfect trading partner. Russia and the US have opposing views on the subject and it has yet to be seen if the situation is an issue that can be resolved. The US feels the Iranian nuclear program is dangerous and will lead to proliferation of weapons. Russia feels that it can abide by the NPT and make money on the program while controlling the fuel cycle. Russia has stated though, that if the IAEA finds Iran to be non-compliant that it will stop its assistance *until Iran has again become compliant.*

A rollback strategy is at best difficult to initiate when Russia will continue to support the Mullahs. The key to a rollback strategy is make the Iranians believe that the program is far too troublesome and expensive to continue. Some of the implied conditions to a proposed resolution in this scenario is the approval by the US of the completion of the Bushehr power plant and a guaranteed fuel agreement with Russia .[172] Perkovich and Manzanero state in the draft *of The Global Consequences of Iran's Acquistion of Nuclear Weapons*, that Russia would be far more likely to back the US and to 'penalize subsequent Iranian acquisition of nuclear weapons if the scenario above was offered and the Iranians refused - opting for their own fuel cycle without outside assistance.

In essence, the Iranians have already refused to cooperate. They have declared that the nuclear fuel from Russia will not be returned and it is their right to establish an indigenous nuclear fuel cycle. Rollback strategy at this point appears to be stalled as only inspections of known nuclear site by the IAEA are currently in place.Again this type of action leads many to believe that Iran will complete its nuclear infrastructure and then withdraw from the NPT to develop and produce nuclear weapons. A firm stance or platform by the US, the EU and Russia needs to be established and implemented *immediately*.

The problem right now is that the EU will trade with Iran and has more or less accepted the fact that Iran will be nuclear capable in the next 6-18months. They seem to be reluctant to adopt any type of rollback or prevention type policy toward Iran regarding nuclear weapons. Countries such as Germany France and Russia were opposed to the war in Iraq. With their demonstrated reluctance to join the political confrontation with a country that they know is breaking international law and is a threat to the world community, it is doubtful that these countries and others from the EU would try to force Iran to rollback its nuclear program. Believing Iran would be willing to rollback its nuclear program and forego its vision of power and influence in the Gulf region is foolish.

So the sanctions imposed by the US, EU and Russia will probably not be a potent weapon in convincing Iran to abandon its nuclear program. Once the Iranians have the nuclear weapons, they will be more than reluctant to dismantle their program. With nuclear weapons in their hands Iran will be able to control the economic life of the Persian Gulf and also indirectly control the energy sector of the industrialized world.

The other motivations for having nuclear weapons need to be explored as well, so that once they have a weapon the containment policy will be tailored to the Iranians foreign policy and potential use of the weapon. Unfortunately, it looks like containment is the most likely strategy that is available and feasible based on today's politics and the reluctance of the Europeans to stop the Iranian nuclear bomb.

Chapter Thirteen
New Cold War and Nuclear
Proliferation - current situation

As it stands now, the current situation of Iran is a continued policy of its quest for nuclear power. The government has stated that it will continue to enrich uranium despite the protests of the US and the EU in blatant disregard for the concern of the IAEA and its demand to agree to additional protocols. Iran is continuing its program on the Bushehr reactors and has declared its intentions to keep the nuclear fuel that Russia has imported and /or will import in the future. This is a dangerous road for the Mullahs to take, as it is a clear sign that they intend to defy the international community, possibly withdraw from the NPT and produce nuclear weapons.

The position of the US is that Iran intends to continue its nuclear energy program while building its nuclear infrastructure to develop and produce nuclear weapons. While the US is not necessarily alone in this attitude, Russia has been opposed to the US strategy of prevention. The EU has become an active partner with the US in the concern that Iran is much closer to be nuclear capable than previously thought. The EU and the

US are closing the gap of ideology on dealing with Iran and have begun to formulate a unified platform to confront Iran on its nuclear program.

Strength in Diplomacy

It is hoped that this situation with Iran can be handled in a diplomatic manner and that all parties will reach a reasonable agreement. However, with the reluctance of Iran to fully and completely disclose its nuclear program and to further explain its inconsistencies to the IAEA - in writing- convinces even the most neophyte student of international affairs that Iran is hiding a nuclear weapons program.

The US and EU have come together on this issue and are pressuring Iran to deal with the UN and the IAEA or face continued US sanctions and EU trade interruptions. Even with increasing international pressure, Iran has not ceded to the IAEA or the international community. On the contrary, it has raised the tension one more notch by declaring its intent to not only continue its nuclear program, but to also complete its indigenous nuclear fuel cycle.

The US does not have direct diplomatic relations with Iran, but through specific communications through the Pakistani Embassy and forums such as the UN, the message is clear - give up the nuclear program or face stiff international penalties. However, given the tenacity of the Islamic Republic's attitude on sponsoring terrorism and pursuing its quest for nuclear weapons despite the threat of international isolation, it appears that Iran may have the infrastructure to produce nuclear weapons within 6-18 months. The diplomatic pressure of the US is unrelenting and will continue. Diplomacy may be taken to the next level if Iran does not respond positively.

"Military force is the final option in terms of diplomacy" states Fox News Analyst CSM Steve Greer.[173] Indeed, von Clausewitz in his treatise "On War" first published in 1832, stated that "War is merely the continuation of [political] policy by other means". Should the multifaceted attempts at peaceful solution fail, the next logical course is to use military force. There are a variety of ways to use military force, but it is most useful in its timing. Even the threat of military force can sometimes bring the opposing parties back to the bargaining table. Diplomacy is a calculating profession that requires an enormous amount of strength, intelligence, politeness, class and eloquence. The use of military force is the final and ultimate option in implementing foreign policy.

A strong presence in Iraq demonstrates that the US is serious about the situation and it is also poised to use its assets to further policy in the region. The President has warned the two most prolific terrorist states in the region, Iran and Syria, that the US will take action if they continue to support terrorism.[174]

Aggressive Mission Oriented Diplomacy by the US and the EU to prevent Iran from obtaining a nuclear weapon capability is paramount. At this point in the Middle East, the balance of power will shift in the wrong direction if the diplomatic avenues fail. With a US presence in Iraq, Iran sees the US as moving in on Islamic soil and with the Mullahs paranoid attitude toward the West, undoubtedly feel the US is a threat. Limited diplomatic engagement may help to strengthen the US position by using the current position of superior power in our favor. The Iranian military is no match for the US, but the US does not wish to invade every country in the region. The potential or actual use of military special operations forces for preemption and interdiction can be a factor in diplomatic engagement.

Strong White house leadership

Whether the leader of this country is a Republican or Democrat, the challenge for the president is clear when it concerns the Global War on Terror and the New Cold War. The country needs to unite against the enemy before it is too late. The GWOT and the New Cold War are both ongoing dynamic challenges that directly concern National Security. The US is on the offensive in the GWOT and it is time to identify the terrorists, the terrorist states and the organizations that support them and formally declare war on the enemies of the United States of America.

After the attacks of September 11, 2001, the need for a unified direction against the enemy terrorists and their sponsoring states was very clear. The US and the Coalition attacked the terrorist bases and eliminated the Taliban from Afghanistan is a swift and decisive campaign. Usama bin Laden and the al Qaeda terrorists were scattered from their home turf and took to hiding in the mountains of Afghanistan and Pakistan. The invasion of Iraq is a strategic maneuver in the GWOT that puts the terrorists on the defensive, increases US presence in the region and puts intentional pressure on Iran. At this point, it should be remembered that Iran is still a major sponsor and producer of international terrorism and the grand strategy for the GWOT appears to have centered on that rogue state.

The worst case scenario in the Middle East is for a terrorist organization or terrorism-sponsor nation to obtain nuclear weapons. In several scenarios involving the proliferation of nuclear weapons, the main reason Iran would try to obtain one is to defend itself against a nuclear Iraq. Whether there was a WMD program that involved nuclear weapons in Iraq or not, Iran thought there had been. So they had an excuse, and a legitimate reason as far as the international realm was concerned (concerning the NPT) to pursue nuclear power and then nuclear weapons. By eliminating the nuclear threat to Iran by invading and dismantling the Iraqi WMD program, Iran has fewer legal reasons to pursue nuclear weapons.

The US military presence in Iraq and Afghanistan has not only put pressure on the terrorists, but has also brought stability to Iran's borders. Without the need to pursue nuclear weapons, Iran will be more likely to comply with the IAEA, the UN and the international community. But because most of the strategy involving Iraq was misunderstood by the American general public, the US has become divided on the issue. While most antagonists feel the war in Iraq has become a quagmire and a major international problem for the US, it has given Iran no choice but to cooperate with the IAEA and the international community. The protagonists view the strategy of limiting Iran's nuclear capabilities and its ability to sponsor terrorism as potent weapon and believe it is working. The President may not reveal the entire strategy on the Global War on Terror, but he has given us the basics for understanding. Iran is part of the "Axis of Evil" and is a target – probably the main target – in the war on terror. President Bush's aggressive policy has turned the tide of the war.

Now its time to go after the individuals that are attempting to continue the attacks on America and the spread of nuclear proliferation in the Persian Gulf. "…the problem predominantly comes to intelligence, the lack of the ability to actually pinpoint where these terrorist organizations are at… or even their cells…Terrorist are very good at providing misinformation…. there are many ways to run into brick walls in trying to determine where these targets are at …" CSM Steve Greer, Special Forces.[175]

To these ends, it is imperative that the United States, not just the present administration, declare war on the terrorists and the terrorist states. Should the party leadership in the White House changes in 4 or 8 or 12 years, the goal of the United States should be the same in regard to the Global War on Terror. If an individual is elected to the Presidency that does not feel the GWOT is the number one priority in America, the enemy will sense weakness and attack. If an administration falters and must rely on other terrorist-appeasing countries to assist the US in this war, the terrorists will strike. The war overseas will then be lost and the enemy will bring the terror war to the US.

As of this writing, the Democratic National Convention is in its 3rd day and there have been several journalists satirizing the security efforts. However, it must be remembered that the terrorists fear a strong America and a strong leader like President Bush. The US is not Spain and will not back down from terrorist attacks even if they try to influence our elections in November 2004.

By the time this book is published the presidential election will be complete. Whoever is elected to the Presidency will find that it is most important to follow the Global War on Terror to its conclusion and to confront Iran aggressively using the five strategies of prevention, preemption, interdiction, rollback/containment and cooperation to end Cold War II.

President Bush realizes that nuclear weapons are not the all-purpose weapons some think they are. These types of weapons are useful for political debate and provocation and at times a deterrent. While Iran may feel that it is cheaper in the long run to build nuclear weapons rather than update and upgrade its conventional forces, they fail to realize that the nuclear weapons cannot substitute for conventional weapons.

In the First Cold War the US and USSR proved that nuclear weapons have no military use other than deterrence, which is actually a political use, and they are completely useless in defense of low-intensity conflicts or unconventional warfare. No nuclear detonations were seen in Vietnam or Afghanistan. Iran appears to be ignorant of this fact and refuses to believe that they may be pursuing a red herring. In response to the deterrence, the enemies of Iran (Israel, Uzbekistan, Turkey, Iraq) may be prompted to produce their own nuclear weapons, thereby *increasing* the risk of war with Iran, rather than preventing it.[176]

The Future

The US stands ready to stop Iran from developing nuclear weapons and Iran will submit to the will of the international community or face isolation. Years ago, isolation would not have been a drastic step in the foreign policy of Iran. But today with its need for European goods, the Iranians are on the brink of a major international breakthrough. Either a breakthrough in trade agreements or a breakthrough in nuclear development.

"The United States was the first to say that Iran was a threat in this way, to try and convince the international community that Iran was trying, under the cover of a civilian nuclear program, to actually bring about a nuclear weapons program," stated National Security Advisor Dr. Condoleeza Rice. "I think we've finally now got the world community to a place, and the International Atomic Agency to a place, that it is worried and suspicious of the Iranian activities," she said. "Iran is facing for the first time real resistance to trying to take these steps".[177]

Diplomatic, political and military options are necessary tools in the deterrence of nuclear weapons in Iran. Diplomatic pressures are constantly being explored through third party negotiations while muddling through the Iranian rhetoric in the UN. Other avenues such as sanctions, embargoes and agreements with other countries that come in economic contact with Iran are essential. President Bush is looking at the possible Iran- 9/11 link as reported by the AP in an article dated July 20, 2004.[178] The US has enemies that are ubiquitous and continuously planning a strategy to covertly attack the US. This could be as complex as conducting "asymmetrical" or multidimensional attacks on almost every aspect of our social, economic and political life as China has attempted,[179] through cyberspace or through a proxy. Iran is no different than other country that desires an end to the United States. Not an end to US foreign policy or an end to US economic presence or an end to Wall street – an end to each American. Be advised – every American is a potential target of the enemy and is at risk. Iran will use its nuclear weapons on the US if it feels it can. The devastating effects of such an attack can only be imagined. The attacks can be avoided with direct action against Iran.

As final course of action, military strikes both overt and covert are also an option in the Second Cold War. A select group of specially trained men from a variety of units in the 1st Special Operations Command have been no doubt planning and rehearsing for operations in Iran. Target systems in the region include communications, manpower, transportation, power and energy networks, and the nuclear power systems. Generally target systems consists of individual targets and may overlap in cause and effect, i.e., a railway station that is destroyed may have been used to transport troops and special supplies such as centrifuges. Destruction of the rail system would impact the two target systems. It is vital to plan for this military contingency now.

Targets in the nuclear energy system include the reactors themselves at Bushehr and Arak, the mines and milling facilities at Yadz, the enrichment facilities at Natanz, Karaj, Sharif, and the Tehran Nuclear Research Center. Even the transportation mechanisms between facilities are targets. After infiltrating the coastline, the Special Operations forces would use laser designators to mark targets for air strikes, destroy command and control centers in the area of operations and possibly use the nuclear scenario against the Iranians by creating damage to the radioactive fuel components and reactor. A vulnerable link in the fuel cycle is fuel fabrication which is conducted at Yadz, Sharif, Bushehr and Araz. An "accident" at the Bushehr reactor building would effectively shut down the area until it was "cleaned up". This is dangerous and potentially risky in the political and diplomatic arena and could alienate the US further from the Arab and non-committal European states. However, interdiction by covert forces can be very effective.

Destroying portions of the nuclear systems that include softer targets such as transportation and communication systems would inhibit the progress, but not prevent it. Eliminating key personnel is also only a temporary solution, but one that can produce results. Attacks in Iran targeting the appropriate systems may be on the horizon.

Senator Joe Biden on The Today Show with Matt Lauer on August 9, 2004 said in a discussion about the relevance of providing addition security for financial institutions in New York, that both sides are right in reference to an imminent threat. Sides? Aren't we all on the same side? Are the politicians in Washington serious? Are they going to politicize the war at every turn? Or are we going to start acting like Americans and win this war?

Iran is not backing down. They have interpreted the lack of action on the part of the European Union and the US as weakness and are going to try to exploit it. They have restarted their equipment to make uranium hexaflouride gas which when used in conjunction with the centrifuges enriches uranium. Low enriched uranium is used in nuclear reactors for power production. Highly enriched uranium is used in producing nuclear bombs. The Iranians have also resumed building centrifuges, despite their promise to not proceed in the "interest of building international goodwill". [180] Retired Lieutenant General Tom MacInerney stated on Fox News Live on Aug 12, 2004 that " Iran has decided to pursue dual purpose technology [procuring uranium hexaflouride gas and building centrifuges]...which means nuclear weapons".

Every country that has stated it was developing a nuclear energy program has attempted to develop nuclear weapons, including the South African program which was later dismantled.[181] It is imperative to stop the Iranian nuclear program before it becomes a never ending deadly nightmare.

The First Cold War was won through persistence, tenacity and using America's strongest asset – its people and our motivation for success. We still have those assets and we should use it to our advantage – our technology, our entrepreneur based economy and our drive for peace and freedom. Iran's oppressive government continues to slow progress in that country and along with the devastating war with Iraq has produced a stagnant, defiant disunified nation. The US and EU must take advantage of their weaknesses. The mind set of the Iranians has got to be understood by the West. The obvious and blatant attempts to mislead the world concerning its nuclear program are painfully obvious and the Iranian government should be held accountable for their actions beginning with written reports. The Iranians have been reporting the status of their nuclear program to the IAEA verbally – which can be easily denied, changed or mismanaged. By using this tactic, the Iranians will continue to have an intermittent uranium enrichment program that they will use as a blackmail weapon. Iran will threaten the continuation of the enrichment process should they not get their way or if they feel the US and EU are coming together on a platform to deal with Iran. The enrichment process needs to stop. This can be accomplished through cooperation between the EU and the US pertaining to trade and monitoring of the Iranian program.

Should Iran be able to continue their nuclear program, it is without a doubt that nuclear weapons will be a reality. The Iranians will feel emboldened and a nuclear exchange between Iran and Israel or New Iraq will be a reality.

Stopping Iran now can avert these cascading events of nuclear war and devastation. Should they obtain nuclear weapons, then a concerted effort to contain their weapons delivery capability should be employed. This includes a regional defense initiative such as missile defense, space-borne platforms to destroy ballistic missiles, cultivation of the growing support of domestic resistance to the Mullahs and special operations troops on the ground inside Iran to disrupt their program.

The international diplomatic players should be, even right now, convincing Iran that the program is too costly, too much trouble and eventually will lead to their destruction. As CSM Steve Greer has stated, the threat is REAL! The case of Iran is much more dangerous and deleterious than Iraq.

As Americans we need to support the President and the military in this fight for freedom. The Democratic and the Republican parties must work together or one of them will be playing into the hands of the enemy.

A combined effort at all levels of government both domestic and abroad should be directed at defeating terrorism and stopping the proliferation of nuclear weapons.

Supreme Leader Khameini and the Mullahs of the Guardian Counsel – you are well advised to stop your nuclear weapons program and cooperate with the world community or prepare for your demise.

Working together as *Americans,* not as Republicans or Democrats, not as progressives or conservatives, but working together to defeat our enemies we can and will win. There is no other alternative.

Steve Greer is a fellow with the National Defense Council Foundation in Alexandria, VA. He is a retired US Army Command Sergeant Major and served in Ranger, Special Forces, and Light Infantry units. He is a member of the Center for Security Policy military committee in Washington, DC.

Steve is a Professor of Special Operations and Low-Intensity Conflict at American Military University and routinely provides expert analysis for FOX News Channel, national public radio, and international print media. Steve is the sole enlisted special military analyst to the Office of the Secretary of Defense and author of the forthcoming *Kin & Strangers: Quelling the Iraqi Insurgency*.

He is a four-time competitor in the grueling Best Ranger Competition and the only Sergeant Major in the world to compete. He received a Master of Arts in Land Warfare and his Doctoral research focuses on the uncertainty of warfare and its implications for reshaping professional enlisted military education policy.

At 33 years of age, he became the youngest Sergeant Major in the U.S. Army. Steve is a life member of the Special Forces Association and National Infantry Association. He lectures throughout the country telling the Army story, advocating a strong national defense, and supporting war-torn children. [182]

Michael (Mick) Schnorr is a concerned citizen and a staunch supporter of the Global War on Terror and defense of the US. The threat of Iran's nuclear proliferation has rekindled his interest in international relations.

Michael is a member of the Academy of Political Science and the National Defense Counsel Foundation. He has earned a bachelor's degree from George Washington University in Physician Assistant Studies, a bachelor's degree from the University of the State of New York in Sociology, a master's degree from the University of Nebraska Medical Center in Family Practice, and a doctorate degree from Pacific Western University in International Relations.

He spent 17 years in the US Military and was a Chief Hospital Corpsman (E7) when he was commissioned as a Naval Officer and Physician Assistant. A combat veteran of Operation Just Cause in Panama, he was assigned to the Marine Corps Security Force Detachment. He also served in the Third Marine Division and First Marine Division in the 1st Reconnaissance Battalion, Headquarters & Service Battalion and the 1st Battalion 1st Marine Regiment Scout Sniper Platoon during the first Persian Gulf War. He was a team corpsman in the Surveillance and Target Acquisition platoon where he was wounded by an exploding rocket propelled grenade in the battle for Al Burgan oil field during combat operations. He also participated in Special Operations in South America.

Michael Schnorr Ph.D. is the founder of Michael Alexander Consulting; International Studies and Observation Group (MAC-I-SOG). He is a member of the Marine Scout Sniper Association, Force Recon Association, the Military Order of the Purple Heart and an associate member of the UDT/SEAL Association.

Glossary

Caliphate - the rulership of Islam; the spiritual head of the Islamic state. In principle, when Muhammad the Prophet died, a caliph or successor was chosen to rule in his place.

Guardian Counsel – the ruling section of the Iranian government first appointed by the Ayatollah Khomeini. The Iranian government is divided into two powers – the secular government of President Khatami is the elected and powerless section. The Mullahs that are appointed to the Guardian Counsel control the IRGC, the nuclear programs, the security of the country and are themselves the Judicial branch, the Legislative branch and the Executive Branch of the government.

IAEA- International Atomic Energy Agency. A division of the United Nations that is responsible for overseeing the nuclear programs of signatory countries.

Imam – In the Shi'a beliefs, the Imam is the religious leader that is able to interpret the Qur'an, and hadiths as it pertains to daily life.

Imamate - is the Leadership or Authority of the Muslim Ummah.

IRGC – Islamic Revolutionary Guards Corps. The military/political arm of the Mullahs. It is divided into 5 sections and its missions include interior security missions to root out opposition and insurgencies that are enemies of the Iranian government; and instigating insurgencies in target countries such as Iraq and Lebanon, while supporting terrorist training and operations targeting Israel and the US.

Kafir – a non-believer of Islam.

Mullahs – Muslim clerics that have attained the experience and religious knowledge to be appointed to the Guardian Counsel.

Shah of Iran – The last Shah of Iran was Reza Pahlavi who was deposed by the Islamic Revolution and Ayatollah Khomeini. The Shah was a strong ally of the US and was abandoned by President Carter in

1979 when the Iranian 'students' attacked the US Embassy in Tehran and held 52 American hostages for 444 days.

Sharia – Islamic law that is strict in its interpretation and application. Thieves are punished by having their hands amputated, etc.

Shi'a – The interpretation of Islam that is prevalent in Iran. The Shi'a Muslims believe in the 7 pillars of faith and are at odds religiously with the Sunnis.

Sunni – The Sunni Muslims are the most in number in the Islamic world. They believe in the 5 pillars of faith and are at odds with the Shi'as. Besides Iran, most Muslims are Sunnis.

Tauhid - Commonly described as Islamic Monotheism. It has three aspects:

(A) Oneness of the Lordship of Allah; *Tauhîd-ar-Rubûbiya*: To believe that there is only one Lord for all the universe, its Creator, Organizer, Planner, Sustainer, and the Giver of security, etc., and that is Allah.

(B) Oneness of the worship of Allah; *Tauhîd-al-Ulûhiya*: To believe that none has the right to be worshipped [e.g. praying, invoking, asking for help (from the unseen), swearing, slaughtering sacrifices, giving charity, fasting, pilgrimage, etc.] but Allah.

(C) Oneness of the Names and the Qualities of Allah: *Tauhîd-al-Asmâ was-Sifât*: To believe that:

(i) We must not name or qualify Allah except with what He or His Messenger SAW has named or qualified Him;

(ii) None can be named or qualified with the Names or Qualifications of Allah; e.g. *Al-Karîm*;

(iii) We must confirm all of Allah's Qualifications which Allah has stated in His Book (the Qur'ân) or mentioned through His Messenger (Muhammad SAW) without changing them or ignoring them completely or twisting the meanings or giving resemblance to any of the created things [e.g. Allah is present over His Throne as mentioned in the Qur'ân (V. 20:5):-

Umma(h) – The Islamic community

Wahabi – A sect of Islam that rose in popularity following the writings of Abd al-Wahab. His teachings were adopted by the House of Saud when they took control of Arabia. The teachings state that the individual Muslim has a direct relationship with Allah and that any other interpretation through a cleric, a friend, a teacher is non-Muslim.

Appendix 1

Chiefs of State and Cabinet Members of Foreign Governments

Last Updated: 2/12/04

Iran---NDE

Supreme Leader	**KHAMENEI,** Ali Hoseini-, *Ayatollah*
President	**KHATAMI-Ardakani,** (Ali) Mohammad, *Hojjat ol-Eslam*
Speaker of the Islamic Consultative Assembly (Majles)	**Mahdavi-KARUBI,** Mehdi, *Hojjat ol-Eslam*
Secretary of the Cabinet	**RAMEZANZADEH,** Abdollah
First Vice Pres.	**AREF-Yazdi,** Mohammad Reza
Vice Pres. For Atomic Energy	**AQAZADEH-Khoi,** Qolam Reza
Vice Pres. For Environmental Protection	**EBTEKAR,** Masumeh
Vice Pres. for Legal & Parliamentary Affairs	**ABTAHI,** Mohammad Ali, *Hojjat ol-Eslam*
Vice Pres. for Physical Training	**MEHR-ALIZADEH,** Mohsen
Vice Pres. for Management & Planning	**SATARI-FAR,** Mohammad
Min. of Agriculture Jihad	**HOJATI,** Mahmud
Min. of Commerce	**SHARIAT-MADARI,** Mohammad
Min. of Communication & Information Technology	**MOTAMEDI,** Ahmad
Min. of Cooperatives	**SUFI,** Ali

Min. of Defense & Armed Forces Logistics	**SHAMKANI,** Ali, *VAdm.*
Min. of Economic Affairs & Finance	**MAZAHERI,** Tahmasb
Min. of Education & Training	**HAZI-QAEM,** Morteza
Min. of Energy	**BITARAF,** Habibollah
Min. of Foreign Affairs	**KHARAZI,** (Ali Naqi) Kamal
Min. of Health, Treatment, & Medical Education	**PEZESHKIAN,** Masud
Min. of Housing & Urban Development	**ABDOL-ALIZADEH,** Ali
Min. of Industries & Mines	**JAHANGIRI,** Eshaq
Min. of Intelligence & Security	**YUNESI,** (Mohammad) Ali, *Hojjat ol-Eslam*
Min. of Interior	**MUSAVI-LARI,** Abdol Vahed, *Hojjat ol-Eslam*
Min. of Islamic Culture & Guidance	**MASJED-JAMEI,** Ahmad
Min. of Justice	**SHOSHTARI,** Mohammad Esmail, *Hojjat ol-Eslam*
Min. of Labor & Social Affairs	**HOSEINI,** Safdar
Min. of Petroleum	**NAMDAR-ZANGANEH,** Bijan
Min. of Roads & Transport	**KHORAM,** Ahmad
Min. of Science, Research, & Technology	**TOWFIQI-Darian,** Jafar
Governor, Central Bank	**SHEIBANI,** Ebrahim
Head of Interest Section in the US	**JAZINI,** Ali
Permanent Representative to the UN, New York	**ZARIF-Khonsari,** Mohammad Javad

*US State Department http://www.cia.gov/cia/publications/chiefs/chiefs83.html

<u>Miltary Officers associated with al Qaeda or the Nuclear Program</u>

IRGC Commander Brigadier-General Rahim Safavi

IRGC Deputy Commander Brig General Baqer Zolqadr

IRGC Former Commander in Lebanon Hossein Mosleh

IRGC Commander Ahmad Vahedi

IRGC Commander Kan'ani

IRGC Commander Naqdi

<u>al Qaeda in Iran</u>

Saif al-Adil

Saad bin Laden

384 al Qaeda terrorists

Appendix 2

Iran's Nuclear facilities

Yadz	Mining, Milling
Isfahan (Esfahan)	Conversion
Karaj, Sharif, Natanz	Uranium,Dual Purpose
Tehran Nuclear Research Ctr	Enrichment
	Centrifuges/gas
Yadz, Sharif, Bushehr, Araz	Fuel Fabrication
TNRC, Other facilties?	Reprocessing Spent
	Uranium into lutonium

Other facilities of importance
Tehran Nuclear Research Center
Bonab Atomic energy Research Center
Esfahan Nuclear Research Center
Fasa: The Rudan Nuclear Research center near Shiraz - Yellow Cake Processing
Lavizan – possible storage site for nuclear weapons or components
Mu'allim Kalayeh – possible research site, confirmed recreation facility for nuclear staff[183]

Endnotes

[1] Taheri, Amir, <u>Recipe for Disaster</u> *National Review Online* November 14, 2003

[2] Jacinto, Leeia, *New Friends, New Ties, Is Iran Supporting al Qaeda?*, ABCNews.com, http://abcnews.go.com/sections/world/goodmorningamerica/iran030522_alqaeda.html

[3] Farideh fahi, *To have or not to have? Irans domestic debate on nuclear options*, Nixon Library www.nixoncenter.org/publications/monographs/Iran%27s%20Nuclear%20Weapons%20Options%20-%20Issues%20and

[4] Al Jazeera Global News, *Nuke Claims, Khatami Chastises US,* March 17, 2004, http://english_aljazeer.net/nr/exeres

[5] Iran's Continuing Pursuit of Weapons of Mass Destruction, US Dept of State Web page, www.state.gov/t/us/rm/33909.htm

[6] Fox News, June 22, 2004 interview with Mark Ginsberg, Steve Pomerantz and Steven Greer

[7] Washington Times, *Iran, Terrorists and Nukes*, May 27, 2004 http://www.washingtontimes.com/functions/print.php?StoryID=20040526-085519-1462r

[8] Stunning Cost of 9/11 Federick u Dicker, New York Post, 1/28/02, www.freerepublic.com/focus/fr/617068/posts

[9] Isaacs, Jeremy and Downing, Taylor, Epilogue: What the Cold War Cost, CNN interactive, www.cnn.com/Specials/cold.war/episodes/24/epilogue/

[10] Worldnet daily Dec 14, 2002 www.wnd.com.news/article.asp?articleID=30003

[11] CIA World Factbook, Iran

[12] Emerick, Yahiya, <u>Understanding Islam</u>, Alpha Books, Indianapolis, Indiana 2002

[13] Lewis, Bernard, The Crisis of Islam, *Holy War and Unholy Terror*, Chapter 1, Modern Library, New York, New York 2003

[14] Mead, John Clark, The New World War, Xulon Press, Fairfax Virginia 2002 Pages 167-168

[15] Emerick, Yahiya, Understanding Islam, pps 306-307,Alpha Books, Indianapolis, Indiana 2002

[16] Tauhid -Allah's Oneness- Az-Zumar: 62, www.java-man.com/Pages/Tauhid/tauhid979824.html

[17] Hamid Algar, Wahhabism: a Critical Essay, pps 32-33, 2002, Islamic Publications International

[18] AFP, *Purported Leader of Al Khobar attacks tells how killers escaped*, Jordan Times, Sunday June 6, 2004, www.aljazeerah.info/news%20archives/2004%20news%20archives/june/6n/purported

[19] Ne-eman, Yisrael, *Saudi Overtures towards Peace*, Mideast On Target, Feb 25, 2002 http://www.me-ontarget.net/archarticles/arch020102/020225saudipeaceovertures.htm

[20] Fighel, Yoni and Shahar, Yaei, *The al Qaeda-Hizballah Connection*, Feb 26, 2002, www.ict.org.il/articles/articledet.cfm?articleid=425

[21] Darling, Dan, *Iranian Force has Long Ties to al Qaeda*, Rantburg, October 14, 2003 www.rantburg.com/poparticle.asp?D=10/14/03&ID=19853

[22] Jacinto, Leeia, *New Friends, New Ties, Is Iran Supporting al Qaeda?*, ABCNews.com, http://abcnews.go.com/sections/world/goodmorningamerica/iran030522_alqaeda.html

[23] Fox News, Iranian Military Unit may be harboring al Qaeda, October 22, 2003

[24] NCRI, *Mullah's Terrorist Training Camps*, www.iranncrfac.org/pages/dossiers/mullahs'%20terrorism/terrorist%20training%20camps.htm

[25] Ibid

[26] Khatami, Official webpage Ministry of Foreign Affairs of the Islamic Republic of Iran http://www.mfa.gov.ir

[27] Pike, John, Qods (Jerusalem) Force Iranian Revolutionary Guard Corps (IRGC-Pasdaran-e Inqilab) www.fas.org/irp/world/iran/qods/

[28] Rantburg 10/14/03, *Iranian Force has long ties to al Qaeda www. rantburg.com*

[29] Fighel, Yoni and Shahar, Yaei, *The al Qaeda-Hizballah Connection*, Feb 26, 2002, www.ict.org.il/articles/articledet.cfm?articleid=425

[30] IBID

[31] Global Security *Iran Report*, 20 October 2003 Volme 6, Number 42 www.globalsecurity.org/wmd/library/news/iran/2003/42-201003_html

[32] Gunaratna, Rohan, Inside al Qaeda, *Global Network of Terror* ppg 12, 74Columbia University Press, New York, New York, 2002

[33] Jacinto, Leeia, *New Friends, New Ties, Is Iran Supporting al Qaeda?*, ABCNews.com, http://abcnews.go.com/sections/world/goodmorningamerica/iran030522_alqaeda.html

[34] Al-Sharq al-Awsat Newspaper 28 February 2003 www.freerepublic.com/focus/nes/854286/posts

[35] Ibid

[36] Ibid

[37] AP, Foxnews, *Iranian military unit may be harboring al Qaeda*, October 22, 2003 www.foxnews.com/story/0,2933,100912,00.html

[38] Michael Ledeen, *The Discovery of Iran*, July 19, 2004, National Review online www.nationalreview.com/ledeen

[39] Isikoff, Michael and Hirsch, Michael *9/11: The Iran Factor, The final report of the 9-11 Commission reveals the troubling new evidence that Tehran was closer to al Qaeda tha Iraq was*, Newsweek National News, MSNBC, July 26, 2004, www.msnbc.msn.com/id/5457389/site/newsweek

[40] Emerick, Yahiya, <u>Understanding Islam</u>, pps 166-169Alpha Books, Indianapolis, Indiana 2002

[41] Spencer, Robert, <u>Onward Muslim Soldiers, *How Jihad still threatens America and the West*</u>, Page 131 Regnery Publishing, Washington DC, 2002

[42] Ibid 132

[43] Venzke, Ben and Ibrahim, Aimee, <u>The al Qaeda Threat, *An Analytical Guide to al Qaeda's Tactics and Targets*</u>, Page 83, Tempest Publishing, Alexandria Virginia, 2003

[44] Emerick, Yahiya, <u>Understanding Islam</u>, pps 350-351 Alpha Books, Indianapolis, Indiana 2002

[45] US Department of State, Background Note:Iran, June2004, Bureau of Near Eastern Affairs, www.state.gov/r/pa/ei/bgn/5314.htm

[46] Henderson, Harry, <u>Global Terrorism, *The Complete Reference Guide*</u>, Page 46-51Checkmark Books, New York, New York, 2001

[47] Gunaratna, Rohan, <u>Inside al Qaeda, *Global Network of Terror*</u> ppg 54 Columbia University Press, New York, New York, 2002

[48] Ibid pps 21-22

[49] Ibid Chapter 1

[50] Federation of American Scientists, World Islamic Front Statement, *Jihad against Jews and Crusaders*, 23 February 1998, http://www.fas.org/irp/world/para/docs/980223-fatwa.htm

[51] Fox News Channel Information, War on Terror, Terror Gorups, al Qaeda, http://www.foxnews.com/waronterror/handbook/flash.html

[52] Venzke, Ben and Ibrahim, Aimee, <u>The al Qaeda Threat, *An Analytical Guide to al Qaeda's Tactics and Targets*</u>, pps 218-230, Tempest Publishing, Alexandria Virginia, 2003

[53] Bowden, Mark, <u>Black Hawk Down, *A Story of Modern*</u> War Atlantic Monthly Press, 1999

[54] Venzke, Ben and Ibrahim, Aimee, The al Qaeda Threat, *An Analytical Guide to al Qaeda's Tactics and Targets*, pps 218-230, Tempest Publishing, Alexandria Virginia, 2003

[55] Gunaratna, Rohan, Inside al Qaeda, *Global Network of Terror* ppg 38 Columbia University Press, New York, New York, 2002

[56] Emerick, Yahiya, Understanding Islam, page 167 Alpha Books, Indianapolis, Indiana 2002

[57] Spencer, Robert, Onward Muslim Soldiers, *How Jihad still threatens America and the West*, Page ix Regnery Publishing, Washington DC, 2002

[58] Planet explorer reference Planetexplorer.discovery.com/ref/history/histottoman.html

[59] The Nizkor Project, *Hamas, Islamic Jihad and the Muslim Brotherhood: Islamic Extremists and the Threat to America*, www.nizkor.org/hweb/orgs/american/adl/hamas/holy-war.html

[60] Fox News Channel Information, War on Terror, Terror Gorups, al Qaeda, http://www.foxnews.com/waronterror/handbook/flash.html

[61] Shaffer, Brenda, *Iran at nuclear threshold*, Armscontrol today, November 2003 www.armscontrol.org/act/2003_11/shaffer.asp

[62] Ibid

[63] Reuters, *IAEA Probes Iran-Pakistan Link, Similar Centrifuges spark concern at UN nuclear agency*, November 27, 2003, www.msnbc.com/news/997702.asp

[64] Charbonneua, Louis, *UN uranium finds links Libya to Iran, Pakistan*, India News June 12, 2004 http://in.news.yahoo.com/040528/137/2dd8w.html

[65] Shaffer, Brenda, *Iran at nuclear threshold*, Armscontrol today, November 2003 www.armscontrol.org/act/2003_11/shaffer.asp

[66] *Implementation of the NPT Safeguards Agreement in the Islamic Republic of Iran*, 18 June 2004, IAEA

[67] *Transcript of Director General's Press Statement on IAEA inspection in Iran*, 18 June 2004, IAEA.org

[68] Eisenstadt, Michael, *Iran's Revolutionary Guard Commander Sends a Warning*, Washington Institutue for Near East Policy, www.washingtoninsititute.org/watch/policywatch/policywatch1998/314.htm

[69] AP, *Iranian Military Unit may be Harboring al Qaeda*, October 22, 2003, Fox News, www.foxnews.com/story/0,2933,100912,00.html

[70] Farideh fahi, *To have or not to have? Irans domestic debate on nuclear options*, Nixon Library www.nixoncenter.org/publications/monographs/Iran%27s%20Nuclear%20Weapons%20Options%20-%20Issues%20and

[71] Iran Press Service, *Rafsanjani says Muslims should use Nuclear Weapon Against Israel*, IPS, December 14, 2001, www.iran-press-service.com/articles_2001/dec_2001/rafsanjani_nuke_threats_141201.htm

[72] Shaffer, Brenda, *Iran at nuclear threshold*, Armscontrol today, November 2003 www.armscontrol.org/act/2003_11/shaffer.asp

[73] EIA.DOE.gov, *Country Analysis Brief: Iran*, www.eia.doe.gov/emeu/cabs/iran.html

[74] Permanent Mission of the Islamic Republic of Iran to the UN, *Why Iran's Nuclear Program is Exclusively Peaceful*, Vienna, November 21, 2003 http://www.un.int/iran/statements/gabodies/

[75] Ibid

[76] Ibid

[77] Large and Associates for Greenpeace UK, *Dual Capable Nuclear Technology* Report Ref No LA RL2084-A, http://archive.greenpeace.org/comms/nukes/nukes.html

[78] Koch, Andrew and Wolf, Jeanette, *Iran's Nuclear Facilties:a Profile*, Center for Nonproliferation Studies, 1998

[79] Shaffer, Brenda, *Iran at nuclear threshold*, Armscontrol today, November 2003 www.armscontrol.org/act/2003_11/shaffer.asp

[80] Large and Associates for Greenpeace UK, *Dual Capable Nuclear Technology* Report Ref No LA RL2084-A, http://archive.greenpeace.org/comms/nukes/nukes.html

[81] Ibid

[82] Nuclear Threat Initiative Iran Nuclear Chronology 14 Feb 2002 http://www.nti.org/e_research/e1_iran_nch_2002.html

[83] Nuclear Threat Initiative *Russia, Iran run N-School Exchange,"* Sunday Times (London), 6 February 2002 http://204.71.60.38/db/nisprofs/russia/exports/rusiran/nukeovr.htm

[84] Nuclear Threat Initiative, Database, Russia:Nuclear Exports to t Iran: Training and Know-How, Updated 24 March 2004, http://204.71.60.38/db/nisprofs/russia/exports/rusiran/nuknow.htm#irnuketrain

[85] Koch, Andrew and Wolf, Jeanette, *Iran's Nuclear Facilties:a Profile*, Center for Nonproliferation Studies, 1998

[86] BBC News UK Edition, *Nuclear Scandal Still begs question*, 5 February 2004, http://news.bbc.co.uk/1/hi/world/south_asia/3464073.stm

[87] Ibid

[88] Institute for War and Peace,Svetlana Moiseeva, Kazakstan: *Nuclear smuggling Fears*, 25 Oct 2002

[89] Nuclear Threat Initiative, *Country Profile, Iran*, http://nti.org/e_research/profiles/Iran/index.html

[90] Center for Nonproliferation studies, Monterey institute of international studies, *weapons of mass destruction in the middle east:Iran*, http://cns.miis.edu/research/wmdme/iran.htm

[91] Ibid

[92] Farideh fahi , *To have or not to have? Irans domestic debate on nuclear options*, Nixon Library www.nixoncenter.org/publications/monographs/Iran%27s%20Nuclear%20Weapons%20Options%20-%20Issues%20and

[93] CNS-MIIS: *Weapons of mass destruction:Iran, Weapons of Mass destruction* Capabilties and Programs http://cns.miis.edu/research/wmdme/iran/htm

[94] Ibid

[95] Ibid

[96] .AP news, *Uranium sneaked past 7 countries and not a single question asked*, www.freerepublic.com/focus/news/746528/posts

[97] *"Border Breach?"* ABC News, 2002, http://abcnews.com/sections/wnt/primetime/sept11_uranium030910.html

[98] AP, Likely 'Dirty Bomb' Material Seized in Ukraine, May 06, 2004, www.foxnews/story/0,2933,119227,00.html

[99] CNN, Official: *US Expels 2 Iranians at UN*, CNN.Com, June 29, 2004, www.cnn.com/2004/US/Northeast/06/29/un.iran/index.html

[100] FAS, Special Weapons Primer, Nuclear Weapons Effects, www.fas.org/nuke/intro/nuke/effects.htm

[101] Ibid

[102] Ibid

[103] Burbach, David, Nuclear Weapons Primer, Nuclear Weapons Introduction, Nov 1997 http://class.lls.edu/spring2003/natsec-manheim/Nuclear_Primer.pdf

[104] National Atomic Museum, Little Boy and Fat Man, Historical Perspectuve www.atomicmuseum.com/tour/dd2.cfm

[105] Burbach, David, Nuclear Weapons Primer, Nuclear Weapons Introduction, Nov 1997 http://class.lls.edu/spring2003/natsec-manheim/Nuclear_Primer.pdf

[106] Ibid

[107] AP, *Iran Test fires New Version of Ballistic Missile*, August 11, 2004, Fox News www.foxnews.com/story/0,2933,128682,00.htm

[108] IRNA, *No world power can overpower the Iranian nation*, Sep 15, www.irna.ir/en/tnews/020915173517.etn00.shtml

[109] Iqbal Siddiqui *The Islamic Revolution in Iran: an inspiration, an and an experiment*, February 1-15, 2000, , Muslim Media www.muslimedia. com/archives/features00/iran-inspire.hmt

[110] MER, *Iran's Reform Dilemma within and against the State*, Middle East Report Online, September 12, 2000, www.merip.org/mero/ mero09100.html

[111] *Amnesty International report on Iran January -December 2003*, www.web.amnesty.org/report2004/irn-summary-eng

[112] Afshin Valinejad *Iran Reform leader shot in Tehran*, March 13, 2000, AP, Seattle Post-Intelligencer

[113] *Sharia*" Encyclopedia of the Orient, http://i-cas.com/e.o/sharia. html

[114] *CIA World Fact book, Iran 2002*

[115] BBC news, *Iran Faces 'Social Explosion'*, 16 may 2002 http:// news.bbc.co.uk/1/hi/world/middle_east/1991684.stm

[116] Golnaz Esfandiari *Generation gap widening in Iran as conservatives try to enforce Islamic codes,* , 12/10/03, Payvands Iran News, www. payvand.com/news/03/dec/1072.html

[117] AP, CBS news, *4,000 Arrests in Iran reform protests* June 28, 2003 http://www.cbsnews.com/stories/2003/06/12/world/main558295.shtml

[118] Ibid

[119] Middle East Media research institute Special dispatch series no 548, August 6, 2003

[120] Emerick, Yahiya, Understanding Islam, pps 350-351 Alpha Books, Indianapolis, Indiana 2002

[121] Henderson, Harry, Global Terrorism, *The Complete Reference Guide*, Page 47Checkmark Books, New York, New York, 2001

[122] Federation of American Scientists, Qods (Jerusalem) Force Iranian Revolutionary Guard Corps (IRGC - Pasdaran-e Inqilab) http://fas.org/irp/ world/iran/qods/

[123] Henderson, Harry, Global Terrorism, *The Complete Reference Guide*, Page 47Checkmark Books, New York, New York, 2001

[124] Khatami President Of The I.R of Iran, Ministry of Foreign Affairs website http://www.mfa.gov.ir

[125] PBS.org, American Experience, Jimmy Carter, People and Events: The Iranian Hostage Crisis, November 1979- January 1981, www.pbs.org/wgbh/amex/carter/peopleevents/e_hostage.html

[126] Dr. Lawrence Grinter, Avoiding the Burden the Carter Doctrine in perspective, Air University Review, January-February 1983, www.airpower.maxwell.af.mil/airchronicles/aureview/1983/jan-feb/grinter.html

[127] Ibid

[128] Parviz Shahnawas, "In Gaudaloupe, Carter announced that Shah must go", VGE, Iran Press Service, www.iran-press-service.com/articles/4toos_vge.html

[129] Dr. Lawrence Grinter, Avoiding the Burden the Carter Doctrine in perspective, Air University Review, January-February 1983, www.airpower.maxwell.af.mil/airchronicles/aureview/1983/jan-feb/grinter.html

[130] The Washington Post, March 10, 2003, Joby Warrick and Glenn Kessler

[131] Nawab Khan, EU-Iran Relations in the last Two Years, 11/23/03, Payvand's Iran News, www. Payvand.com/news/03/nov/1139/html

[132] Perkovich, Manzanero, *The Global Consequences of Iran's Acquisition of Nuclear Weapons*, The Nixon Center, 2004

[133] Public Law 104-172- Aug 5 1996, Iran and Libya Sanctions Act of 1996

[134] Perkovich, Manzanero, *The Global consequences of Iran's acquisition of Nuclear Weapons*, Nixon Library 2003

[135] *Amnesty International report on Iran January -December 2003,* www.web.amnesty.org/report2004/irn-summary-eng

[136] Khan, Nawab *EU-Iran relations in the last two years,* 11/23/03, www.payvand.com/news/03/nov/1139.html

[137] Ibid

[138] Coulter, Ann, <u>Treason, *Liberal Treachery from the Cold War to the War on Terorism,*</u> Page 37Crown Forum, New York , 2003

[139] Robert Morton Ed, Woldnetdaily Geostrategy-Direct Intelligence Brief, US Intel:WMD went to Syria Last Year, January 30, 2004 www.worldnetdaily.com/new/article.asp?ARTICLE_ID=36844

[140] Robert Morton Ed, Woldnetdaily Geostrategy-Direct Intelligence Brief, New Evidence:Saddams WMD in Lebanon, May 20, 2004 www.worldnetdaily.com/news/article.asp?ARTICLE_ID=38581

[141] AIPAC, *Circle of Terror,* Near East Report, July 29, 2002 www.aipac.org/documents/circlener072902.html

[142] Ahavat Israel, *Wars in Israel,* www.ahavat-israel.com/ahavat/eretz/wars.asp

[143] United Nations Security Counsel Resolution 242, Nov 22, 1967, Copyright 1996, The Avalon Project at Yale Law School, www.yale.edu/lawweb/Avalon/un/un242.htm

[144] Ahmed Rashid, Jihad the Rise of Militant Islam in Central Asia, Penguin Books, Yale University 2002 Pages 218-221

[145] MIlitants in Europe Openly call for Jihad and the Rule of Islam, April 26, 2004, The New York Times, Forign Desk, Tyler, Van Natta, http://query.nytimes.com/gst/abstract.html?res=f10f10fb3b5e0c758eddad0894dc404482

[146] Europe Fears threat from its converts to Islam, International Herald Tribune, July 19, 2004, www.freerepublic.com/focus/f-news/1175543/posts

[147] BBC News World Edition, 'Shoe Bomber' jailed for life, 30 January 2003, www.bbc.co.uk/2/hi/Americas/2708205

[148] Rohan Gunaratna, Inside al Qaeda, *Global network of Terror*, Columbia University Press 2002 page 115

[149] Stunning Cost of 9/11 Federick u Dicker, New York Post, 1/28/02, www.freerepublic.com/focus/fr/617068/posts

[150] Hannity, Sean, Deliver US From Evil, *Defeating Terrorism, Despotism and Liberalism*, Page 287 ReganBooks, 2004

[151] Kawach, Nadim, *Iran Makes Big Strides in Missile Capabiltiy*, Benador Associates, 2004, http://www.benadorassociates.com/article2690

[152] Ibid

[153] Al Jazeera Global News, *Nuke Claims, Khatami Chastises US*, March 17, 2004, http://english_aljazeer.net/nr/exeres

[154] Ibid

[155] Al Jazeera Global News, US Hawks Blocking Normalisation with Iran, March 17, 2004, http://english+aljazeer.net/nr/exeres

[156] Taheri, Amir, Recipe for Disaster *National Review Online* November 14, 2003

[157] Ibid

[158] Ibid

[159] Bowden, Mark, Blaackhawk Down, A Story of Modern War, Page 333 Atlantic Monthly Press, New York, 1999

[160] Taheri, Amir, Recipe for Disaster *National Review Online* November 14, 2003

[161] Rashid, Ahmed, Jihad, *The Rise of Militant Islam in Central Asia*, 101-106, Penguin Books, New York, 2002

[162] Hannity, Sean, Deliver US From Evil, *Defeating Terrorism, Despotism and Liberalism*, Page 295 ReganBooks, 2004

[163] Ibid

[164] Venzke, Ben and Ibrahim, Aimee, The al Qaeda Threat, *An Analytical Guide to al Qaeda's Tactics and Targets*, page 108, Tempest Publishing, Alexandria Virginia, 2003

[165] CNN Cold War, Episode 16: Détente, 1998 http://www.cnn.com/SPECIALS/cold.war/episodes/16/

[166] Hannity, Sean, Deliver US From Evil, *Defeating Terrorism, Despotism and Liberalism*, pps77-80 ReganBooks, 2004

[167] Ibid

[168] Perkovich, Manzanero, *The Global Consequences of Iran's Acquisition of Nuclear Weapons*, The Nixon Center, 2004

[169] Taheri, Amir, Recipe for Disaster *National Review Online* November 14, 2003

[170] FAS, Weapons of Mass Destruction, *WMD Around the World, Iraq Osiraq/Tammuz 1* http://www.fas.org/nuke/guide/iraq/facility/osiraq.htm

[171] CDI Nuclear Issues, FACT SHEET: North Korea's Nuclear Weapons Program http://www.cdi.org/nuclear/nk-fact-sheet.cfm

[172] Perkovich, Manzanero, *The Global Consequences of Iran's Acquisition of Nuclear Weapons*, The Nixon Center, 2004

[173] Fox News, June 22, 2004 interview with Mark Ginsberg, Steve Pomerantz and Steven Greer

[174] Bush cautions Iran and Syria, BBC World News, July 21, 2003, http://news.bbc.co.uk/2/hi/Americas/3084213.htm

[175] Fox News, June 22, 2004 interview with Mark Ginsberg, Steve Pomerantz and Steven Greer

[176] Shahram Chubin, Iran's Strategic Environment and Nuclear Weapons, The Nixon Library

[177] Kirtz, Julie and AP, US Considering to Deter Iran, N. Korea, August 08, 2004, Fox News, www.foxnews.com/story/0,2933,128387,00.html

[178] AP, Bush Looks at Possible Iran-Sept 11 Link, July 20, 2004, Fox News, www.foxnews.com/story/0,2933,126206,00.html

[179] Colonels Qiao Liang and Wang Xiangsui , Unrestricted Warfare, Pan American Publishing Company; August 22, 2002,

[180] AP, Diplomats:Ian Resuming Nuke Work, Fox News July 28, 2004, www.foxnews.com/story/0,2933,127310,00.html

[181] CNS, MIIS, CNS Resources on South Africa's Nuclear Weapons ProgramSouth Africa's Nuclear Weapons Program: An Annotated Chronology, 1969-1994 http://cns.miis.edu/research/safrica/chron.htm

[182] The Greer Foundation, http://www.thegreerfoundation.org

[183] Rubin, Michael, Irans Burgeoning WMD Program, Middle East Intelligence Bulletin Mar-Apr 2002 http://www.rezapahlavi.com/articles/meib-april.html

www.ingramcontent.com/pod-product-compliance
Lightning Source LLC
Chambersburg PA
CBHW020412290526
45785CB00002B/531